HERE, NOW, AND ALWAYS

Voices of the First Peoples of the Southwest

HERE, NOW, AND ALWAYS
Voices of the First Peoples of the Southwest

Compiled and edited by Joan K. O'Donnell

Text by **Carlotta Penny Bird**, Santo Domingo Pueblo

Tony R. Chavarria, Santa Clara Pueblo

Anthony Dorame, Tesuque Pueblo

Gloria Emerson, Diné (Navajo)

Rex Lee Jim, Diné (Navajo)

Angelo Joaquin, Jr., Tohono O'odham (Pima)

Leigh J. Kuwanwisiwma, Hopi

Michael Lacapa, Apache/Hopi/Tewa

Edmund J. Ladd, Zuni Pueblo

Lillie Lane, Diné (Navajo)

Tessie Naranjo, Santa Clara Pueblo

Paula Rivera, Taos Pueblo

Luci Tapahonso, Diné (Navajo)

Veronica E. Velarde Tiller, Jicarilla Apache

With a Foreword by **Rina Swentzell**

Introduction by **Bruce Bernstein**

Museum of New Mexico Press   Santa Fe

The publication is based on the exhibition *Here, Now, and Always*: *Voices of the First Peoples of the Southwest*, conceived and organized by Bruce Bernstein for Museum of Indian Arts and Culture, Santa Fe.

The publication of this book was made possible by a generous grant from the Friends of Indian Art, a support group of the Museum of Indian Arts and Culture, Santa Fe.
Support for the exhibition was provided by the National Endowment for the Humanities.

Major contributors to the *Here, Now, and Always* exhibition included Nancy and Richard Bloch; Maggy Ryan Charitable Trust; the Marshall L. and Perrine D. McCune Charitable Foundation; Charles and Valerie Diker; The Donald Pitt Family Foundation; Eileen A. Wells; and the estate of Jordie Chilson.

Project Director: Mary Wachs
Design and Production: Mary Sweitzer Design
Composition: Set in Futura Condensed Light with Futura Condensed Bold Display

Manufactured in Hong Kong
10 9 8 7 6 5 4 3 2 1

Library of Congress Cataloging-in-Publication Data Available ISBN 0-89013-387-5 (P).

MUSEUM OF NEW MEXICO PRESS
Post Office Box 2087
Santa Fe, New Mexico 87504
Photos page 2 (41); 6–7 (70–71); 8 (47).

I am here.

I am here, now.

I have been here, always.

—Edmund J. Ladd, Zuni Pueblo

Here, Now, and Always

is dedicated to

Edmund J. Ladd (1926—1999)

CONTENTS

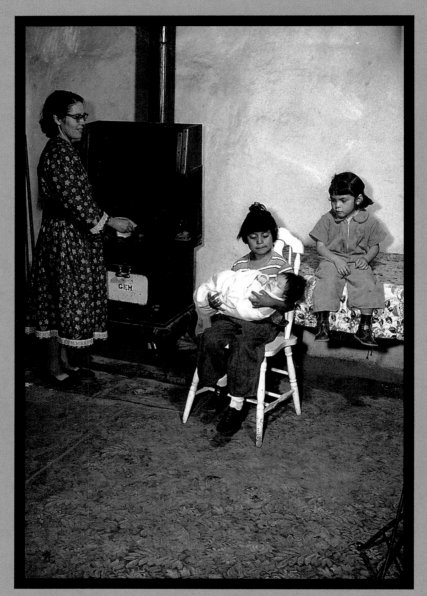

Cochiti Pueblo, ca. 1950

FOREWORD

It is a snowy January evening. The piñon trees, laden with white, are bending to touch the earth. No tracks yet in the fresh snow. Grasses, small bushes, rocks, and uneven surfaces hide under a smooth, glistening blanket of white. I breathe in deeply and feel the beauty of the place flow through me.

And, so, I think of how I need such moments to remind me of the sacred within and around me. On other evenings my spirit can blossom with the red clouds glowing in the setting sun. Our place, this Southwest, has no lack of the sublime. Native peoples have reveled in its profound intensity for centuries.

In these pages are words of Native peoples of the Southwest remembering the thoughts and perceptions of our ancestors in which the beauty of life and place is acknowledged. They talk about the emergence from the womb of the Earth Mother, moving from darkness into the light of the Father Sun. They talk about traveling and searching for the center place alongside lightning, sacred clouds, rainbows and water spiders. They remember that the center place is where prayers and songs of thankfulness for the mountains, the rain, the deer, and the clouds are given to the breath of the cosmos. They also remember that transformation is in our very next step, much as clouds transform before our eyes.

As clouds shift and seasons change, so do human thoughts and human-made processes. As Ed Ladd writes in this text, "There is a season for growth . . . a season for caring . . . a time for resting." The process of birthing, tending and nurturing the Here, Now and Always exhibition also came with intense moments of moving through exhilarating insights, depressing frustrations, and deepening friendships. For me, human relationships are the most difficult. As I lived through the conceptualization process of the exhibit with others, I had to remind myself that the struggle for balanced relationships among all aspects of life — mountains, plants, and animals, including other humans — is the central issue of life for my ancestral Pueblo people. This helped me understand that the process of creating the exhibit was like living everyday life with all its frustrations, angers, delights, and joys.

I relish the words included in this book. These words are like the snow covering the uneven ground, bringing unity, inspiration, and sublimity into our lives. They remind us of the creativity and beauty inherent in human thought and activity, which, in Pueblo terms, are extensions of the place wherein we dwell.

—Rina Swentzell, Santa Clara Pueblo

INTRODUCTION

Museums in North America and Western Europe historically have presented the authoritative view of the "expert" outsider looking in and "explaining" Native histories and cultures, portraying Indian and other indigenous peoples as something out of the past and fixed in time. Today, museums are challenged to reconsider this approach. *Here, Now, and Always,* a book based on an exhibition at the Museum of Indian Arts and Culture in Santa Fe, New Mexico, was conceived to redress the flawed perspective of the past by allowing the Native peoples of the Southwest to be accessible through their own words and viewpoints. We wanted to uncover existing stories rather than create new ones, to organize the book around Native worldviews and philosophies, and to demonstrate the active role of Native peoples in shaping their own cultures and lives.

We began planning Here, Now, and Always in 1989. The project was intended to help transform the new Indian Arts museum into both an active curatorial and exhibition space and a place of living peoples. Early in the planning process, the exhibit's curatorial committee resolved not to structure the exhibit according to Western categories of time lines or tribes. As Ed Ladd joked, with a serious edge, "We didn't want to put on display the corn, beans, and squash Indians. And no

flute music!" Instead, we decided to tell the complex stories of Native peoples' lives and histories from a Native point of view, organized around Native principles and ideas.

This book features a selection of words of fourteen Native writers who were key contributors to the exhibition, which included more than two hundred individual voices in written text, audio, and video formats. In the exhibition, Native writers, artists, community activists, elders, scholars, and students from throughout the Southwest—Navajos (Diné), Utes, Apaches, Pueblos, Mojaves, Tohono O'odhams (Pimas), and others—relate different cultural traditions and personal experiences, together conveying the texture of real people's lives. Their voices demonstrate persuasively that we can know and understand the past and present only through our individual or collective contemporary experiences. Using words from Native peoples of the present, the exhibition and this book illuminate the uses and meaning of ancestral objects, creating the sense of continuity inherent in contemporary Native cultures.

A museum exhibition or a book can never fully stand in for Indian people or communities but we hope this text and its accompanying images will promote understanding of the multilayered Native worldview, rejecting the anthropological overlay familiar to the non-

Native world. The book gives equal weight to diverse voices and objects that tell stories — not concise, "scientific" tales but frameworks for understanding behaviors and worldviews.

Native peoples of the Southwest have their own unique and enduring concept of the world. At a ceremonial dance today in any one of the pueblos, you will see people dancing the Creation at the very spot of Creation, the Emergence Place. The dance is not a symbolic re-creation of that historical or mythological moment but rather an act of Creation itself, ongoing, in which the people of today, along with today's animals and elements and landforms, all participate. People are dancing on the same ground where they have danced for a thousand years or more, dressed as they have been dressed since at least the fourteenth century but with today's Nikes.

This sense of the continuity of tradition, and the knowledge that tradition also involves change, is at the core of *Here, Now, and Always*. Native people at any one moment stand *inside* their history, and that history is continuous because the Creation is ongoing. Given this, it is unremarkable, not dissonant, for an Indian elder to speak English or Tewa, Spanish or Navajo, for an Indian teenager to dance the Corn Dance and to drink Coca-Cola, for an Indian woman to weave a blanket of handspun wools and to sell it through her website on the Internet.

The enduring cultures of southwestern Indian peoples are worth celebrating for their strength and survival in the face of continuing adversity. Foreign forms of education, religion, food, housing, transportation, entertainment, clothing, and disease have had a profound impact on Native peoples, becoming part of their ethos. *Here, Now, and Always* is designed to convey something of the experiences that Native peoples of the Southwest have had over the four hundred years since the Spanish conquest, and over the two millennia preceding the arrival of Europeans.

The "Earth Words" that follow, created by Ed Ladd and Luci Tapahonso, are thematic threads that lead the reader through a cultural landscape, breathing life from the Creation into the objects illustrated here, carrying us from the distant mythological past across space and time to today.

The parting message of Here, Now, and Always is one of survival. Ed Ladd, who selected the title for the exhibit, wished to convey to visitors that Native peoples of the Southwest did not come here from somewhere else but have been here since the beginning. To hear and to read the words of the first peoples of the Southwest arouses a stirring and profound understanding about their histories and cultures.

Bruce Bernstein,
Assistant Director for Cultural Resources,
National Museum of the American Indian

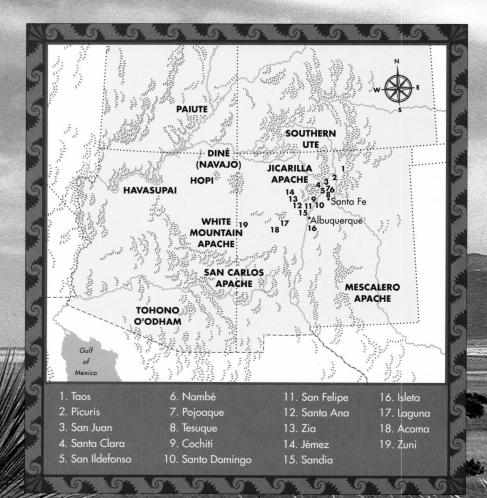

PAIUTE

SOUTHERN
UTE

DINÉ
(NAVAJO)

JICARILLA
APACHE

HOPI

HAVASUPAI

1

2
3
4 5 7 6
8
14
13
12 11 10
15
17
18 16

Santa Fe

Albuquerque

19

WHITE
MOUNTAIN
APACHE

SAN CARLOS
APACHE

MESCALERO
APACHE

TOHONO
O'ODHAM

Gulf
of
Mexico

1. Taos	6. Nambé	11. San Felipe	16. Isleta
2. Picuris	7. Pojoaque	12. Santa Ana	17. Laguna
3. San Juan	8. Tesuque	13. Zia	18. Acoma
4. Santa Clara	9. Cochiti	14. Jémez	19. Zuni
5. San Ildefonso	10. Santo Domingo	15. Sandia	

Map: Peoples of the greater Southwest region.
Background: The llanos extending to the Animas Range,
New Mexico.

In the beginning,
The earth was soft,
There were no humans,
There was no laughter.
Born of Mother Earth
And Father Sun,
Are the humans.
It is the Word
Of the beginning.
—Edmund J. Ladd, Zuni Pueblo

PART I: **ANCESTORS**

Peoples of the Southwest trace their origins to the Earth Mother. Pueblos, Navajos (Diné), Apaches, Utes, Paiutes, Tohono O'odhams, and the other Native peoples of the region are inextricably linked to the land in which they live. Alive with sacred places and sacred stories, the land represents the past and future of the tribes. It is central to all oral histories, to family ties, to the sources of plants and animals and the uses of minerals, to the shape of architecture and the structure of communities. It is the heart of ceremony and religion. It is where an understanding of the peoples of the Southwest must begin. The land itself is the original ancestor.

The relationship of people to land is not only symbolic. It is tangible in daily life, as vital today as it was two thousand years ago. For the archaeologist, too, the land yields information critical to understanding how earlier people lived. Articles fashioned from local materials — clays, fibers, animal skins, and stones — provide clues to the lifeways of the ancient indigenous peoples of each region, to how they used the resources of and adapted to their environment. It is here, among the ancestors, that we begin to recognize the connections between the Southwest and the rest of North and Central America. These links can be seen in the horned serpent imagery found in Mesoamerican temples, in two-thousand-year-old rock art in the mountains of Chihuahua, and on the pottery made by twenty-first-century residents of the pueblo of San Ildefonso. They are apparent in the Southern Plains–style beaded deerskin dress worn by a Mescalero Apache girl in southern New Mexico. Vividly, the words of today's Native peoples as they reflect on their heritage open the door to the ancient worlds and

Pueblo Bonito, Chaco Culture National Historic Park, New Mexico

Wupatki Pueblo, Wupatki National Monument, Arizona.

lasting connections of the American Southwest.

The peoples' ancestral homelands follow the great river courses: the Salt and the Gila, the Rio Grande, the San Juan and Colorado rivers. These rivers trace paths through several different geographic areas — high and low desert, basin-and-range, mountain and riverine — and the environment of each has influenced the adaptations of the people who live there. In southeastern Arizona, the first sedentary villages of the region were built by the ancient Hohokam and Salado cultures. They constructed an extensive and sophisticated network of irrigation canals, walled adobe villages, and impressive ceremonial ballcourts. Their descendants, the Tohono and Akimel O'odhams, still harvest the fruit of the Saguaro cactus and grow the tepary beans their ancestors cultivated some two thousand years ago.

Then, as now, the region was a corridor for travel and trade, linking greater Mesoamerica, California, the desert West, and the greater Southwest.

The greater Southwest, encompassing the Great Plains to the east, the Great Basin to the north,

Coiled Mogollon storage basket from New Mexico's Guadalupe Mountains, ca. 1200–1425.

Wupatki Pueblo

and extending west to California, was first peopled by Paleo-Indian big-game hunters who used large Clovis points and atlatls to hunt mastodons and bison and left their record in caches of blades and chert nodules. The Rio Grande region was an exception to the hunting-gathering that characterized the regions around it with its early commitment to farming. The corridor was a life-line for cultural exchange, giving rise to the community of Paquimé (Casas Grandes) in northern Chihuahua around A.D. 1200, and such valuables as copper bells, marine shells, and parrots passed this way, along with the ideas and beliefs of cultures far to the south. The Zuni people today tell of how, in ancient times, their relatives traveled here from the north to found Paquimé.

The Mogollon Highlands, encompassing a large portion of southwest New Mexico, southeastern Arizona, and north-

ern Mexico, is an area rich in natural resources and the location of the headwaters of the Salt and Gila Rivers. Characterized by wooded mountains and small, lush stream valleys, the highlands were the site of important indigenous developments in hunting and gathering, irrigation farming, and pottery. The renowned black-and-white Mimbres pottery was made here, as were textiles and sandals created from yucca fibers.

North of the Mogollon lies the Four Corners region conjoining Utah, Colorado, New Mexico, and Arizona. This is the heart of the Colorado Plateau, a geologically diverse area that features of snowcapped San Juan Mountains and its progeny, the San Juan River at its northern reach and, to the south, the dry and formidable San Juan Basin with Chaco Canyon at its center. The arid canyon was home to the extraordinary Chaco phenomenon (ca. A.D.

The Rio Grande at Kuaua, Coronado
State Monument, New Mexico.
Inset: Pueblo Bonito, Chaco Culture
National Historic Park.

860-1130), the florescence of a sedentary ancestral Pueblo culture whose elaborations included monumental multistoried masonry architecture, exceptional black-and-white pottery, and a far-reaching trade system evidenced in rich caches of turquoise beads and imported feather and shell artifacts that continue to be a source of fascination to archaeologists and of pride to the Pueblo people who recognize their ancestry at Chaco. More recently the area has been home to the once-nomadic Navajos, whose oral history animates the land with the sacred beings who created and settled it.

North of the San Juan Basin lay the San Juan Uplands, a region of green mesas, abundant springs, and perennial streams. With the collapse of the Chaco culture in the twelfth century, Chaco people migrated outward to the region's periphery. To the north the results included the architecturally grand cliff dwellings at Mesa Verde (A.D. 1200-1300). There, the kiva, a key architectural and ceremonial feature of today's pueblos, was developed. The pottery making that flourished here during the relative brevity of its occupation continues among the Pueblos today, whose origin and clan stories are embedded in the local landscape and in the adjoining Upper Rio Grande area.

The Upper Rio Grande Valley, home to the modern Pueblo people, is the longstanding connection between the Southwest and the Great Plains to the east. With its varied geography, it was simultaneously home to early sedentary farmers and nomadic hunter-gatherers and a corridor along which great population movements took place over vast stretches of time. Since the fourteenth century, Pueblo Indians have occupied villages along the great river. Apache settlements nestle nearby, and large trade fairs attract Native neighbors from the Plains. The stories told here today invoke the legacy of the past.

"Listen carefully. Let the stories carry you to the center created by each Native community. Here, at the intersection of sky and earth, you will find the Southwest's people (Sarah Schlanger)."

ORIGINS

Spruce Tree House cliff dwellings at Mesa Verde, Colorado.

Pueblo people believe that our origins are within Earth Mother. We are literally born of the earth and can mark the places in the land from which we came. These places are generally watery places, springs or lakes. They are also places that connect us to the other levels of existence. Our origins are where we began and where we return. We were born of the mother and return into the earth upon death.

All existence swirls around the center. The houses of the people, the hills and mountains, are in concentric circles around the center place. The sky and earth define the sphere within which the center is crucial to the orientation of the whole. The breath of the universe passes through this center place, as did our people when they emerged into this level of life.

I am happiest when I revisit the ruins of my Pueblo ancestors and imagine the struggles and joys of their lives in the many places that they lived. Chama, Galisteo, and the Northern Rio Grande region were home to my ancestors. They adapted to the landscape, the waterways and rain patterns. Movement did not stop. My ancestors

Left: Micaceous lidded cooking pot made by Virginia Romero, Taos Pueblo, 1950s. Right: Black-on-white pitchers and mugs from the Chaco Canyon and Mesa Verde areas, ca. 1000–1300.

continued to move about from place to place acquiring an intimate knowledge of the hills and valleys of this gentle, yet harsh, land.

Mesa Verde is an exquisitely beautiful place. Our ancestors lived in sandstone cliff shelters located high in the piñon- and juniper-studded canyons of the region. Within the cliff shelters, the ancestors built houses and storage rooms of readily available sandstone. They planted their fields on the tops of the mesas and down below in the canyon areas. From their magnificent shelters, they spoke to the clouds and waited for the rains to bring water for them and their corn, bean, and squash plants.

— Tessie Naranjo, Santa Clara Pueblo

Together we traveled,
in search of the center place.
In numbers we grew.
The center place had not been found.
The gods divided the people.
Some traveled north,
to the land of winter.
Some to traveled south,
to the land of summer.
We are the people.

— Edmund J. Ladd, Zuni Pueblo

Top: Chihuahua polychrome effigy pot from Casas Grandes (Paquimé), ca. 1200–1425.
Bottom: White House Ruin at Canyon de Chelly National Monument, Arizona.

Rock art at Village of the Great Kivas, New Mexico.

We, the Zuni, traveled as a single family from the place of the beginning to search for our center place. In time, we increased in numbers, so the gods separated and divided the family. There is a place in present-day central Arizona called "The Place Where the People Divided." Some traveled to the east and north to the great river and beyond. Others traveled south beyond the mountains of perpetual snow. Still others went to the land of the macaw, which is also known as the land of eternal summer. They are our relatives. Without a doubt, some of our relatives who traveled south were the people who built and occupied Paquimé.

In the words of our elders, our universe that we share with the spirit beings extends to the four corners of the world and to the four encircling oceans. It extends from the mist-enshrouded and moss-draped mountains to the springs and rivers of the valleys. Within these mystical boundaries is the "Place of the Beginning." It is in the Grand Canyon near a place called "Ribbon Falls." The route of travel, east and northward, is marked by many named places now in ruins, such as Walnut Canyon, Winona, Sunset Crater, Canyon Diablo, White House, Aztec, Village of the Great Kivas, and, finally, the Center Place, modern-day Zuni Pueblo.

—Edmund J. Ladd, Zuni Pueblo

Archaeologists, geologists, ethnohistorians, and other researchers are collecting fascinating evidence from the middle Colorado and Little Colorado river areas regarding the human evolutionary history of North America. This region is important to the Hopi people, for it is the heartland of our aboriginal lands. Among the footprints are ancestral Hopi villages, burial sites, sacred trails and springs, petroglyphs, pictographs, and sacred sites. In my visits to the numerous archaeological sites in this area, I have observed evidence of villages once occupied by different Hopi clans. I believe it is accurate to say that our history goes back at least ten thousand years.

The Hopis call Pueblo Bonito "The Place Beyond the Horizon." In our Hopi migration stories, Pueblo Bonito and other villages in the valley were resting places for many clans prior to their final journey to the mesas. Clans that have ancestral ties to the region include the Parrot, *Katsina,* Sparrow-Hawk, Squash, Crane, Bow, Sand, Lizard, and Eagle. When I visit the area, I feel its mystery and significance. Pueblo people still pay spiritual homage to this "footprint," for no archaeological site is ever considered abandoned. Pueblo Bonito is still a living legacy to us and to other Pueblo people.

Pueblo Bonito, Chaco Canyon.

Why is the Grand Canyon important to Hopi people? The answer is simple: We *are* the canyon. The Grand Canyon is both the genesis and the final destination of our people. It is our beginning because our emergence to the Fourth Way of Life occurred there. It is our destination because when a Hopi completes the human life cycle, the canyon becomes his or her final spiritual home. We are the canyon.

The *Katsina* represent a set of beliefs centered around the environment and the relationship between man and nature. This word is of Hopi origin and literally translates to "life," but it reflects a deeper philosophy. In clan traditions, these spirit beings helped the Hopi survive during the migration period. Today, *Katsina* belief is expressed in different ways. *Katsina* spirit beings still visit the pueblos and hold dances. They act as messengers of prayer to all the forces of nature and the universal environment.

—Leigh J. Kuwanwisiwma, Hopi

Gobernador Knob sits at the center of Dinétah (Navajoland). On top of this sacred mountain, we are centered in the universe and balanced in life. Changing Woman, the Navajo goddess, was born here. The idea of embracing and mastering change began on top of this mountain. This is our place of origin. We came together here and are still in the process of becoming a people. Before, as hunters and gatherers, we lived in instability and were unorganized. At *Dinétah* we acquired a sense of purpose and a reason for being. We learned ceremonial, economic and social systems that allowed us to prosper as a people, to endure hardships and always come out the winner. *Dinétah* will always be the sacred center for us.

—Rex Lee Jim, Diné

Creation of North Sacred Mountain, by Harrison Begay, Navajo, 1957.

The Holy People lived here in the beginning.
They built the first "hooghan," made the first weapons,
sang the first songs, and the first prayers.
Diné language, ceremonies,
history, and beliefs began here.
This is where we began.

—Luci Tapahonso, Diné

Mythology basket made by Sally Black, Navajo, 1988.
Western White Mountain

Clan origin stories are part of a Navajo woman's social bundle. 'Asdzáá Nádleehí (Changing Woman) was lonely, so she created four or five clans. She set them on western shores and directed them homeward with special powers. As the ancestors traveled, they took on names inspired by accidents. One ancestor struck bitter water, hence the Tódí ch'íínii (Bitterwater) clan was born. Battling many elements, they wearily traveled about, wanting to retrace their steps. 'Asdzáá Nádleehí disapproved and conferred with the deities to perform a ritual. Diyin Dine'é did as instructed but lost a cane. 'Asdzáá Nádleehí made them repeat the ritual by expanding a set of prayers. Other clans were added, naming themselves for a sacred mark or cosmic event, and still others were adopted from other tribes.

— Gloria Emerson, Diné

The earliest memory we have of Tsébiyahanii'áhí (Chaco Canyon) is in this condensed story: Náá'íilbįįhí (Gambler) descended into Chaco Canyon. He tricked the Pueblo people into gambling and won them and their property. The Navajo came to gamble, and they, too, lost. Náá'íilbįįhí wanted more, so he ordered his slaves to build a great village, but the slaves aligned with Jaa'báni, Tł'ííshtsoh, and Na'azísí (Gopher Bat, Great Snake, and Gopher). Niłch'í Dine'é diverted Náá'íilbįįhí's attention by acting indifferent to his stakes until Náá'íilbįįhí offered himself. Niłch'í Dine'é won, and all were freed. He placed Náá'íilbįįhí on an arrow and shot him into the sky. Náá'íilbįįhí mumbled a strange language as he ascended and was never seen in this form again.

— Gloria Emerson, Diné

Western White Mountain Apache basketry bowl with human, animal, and bird figures, ca. 1930.

The center of the Tohono O'odham universe, Baboquivari Peak in Arizona.

The Hohokam, "Those who are gone," gave present-day desert dwellers in southern Arizona many gifts, including the tepary, a cultivated bean. The desert people, the O'odham, continue the farming legacy begun by the Hohokam by growing tepary beans, cotton, corn, and other arid-land crops. This knowledge of traditional farming practices, crops and seeds helped and continues to help the O'odham survive as a unique group.

"Baboquivari Peak is the center of the universe." From there, *I'itoi,* or Elder Brother, watches out over the O'odham, the people of southern Arizona. Our elders advise us to make the trip to *I'itoi's* home at least four times in our lifetime, with gifts of thanks for our safety. We also renew our commitment to live as respectful community members. The Baboquivari mountain range provides rain runoff for the crops of the few traditional farmers left today. In our pilgrimages, we ask Elder Brother for this runoff to irrigate our crops. Despite the decline in farming, many tribal members still make the pilgrimage to the mountain to pay respect to *I'itoi.*

— Angelo Joaquin, Jr., Tohono O'odham

THE ELEMENTS

*P**ueblo people believe that clay has life.*** A sacred relationship between the potter and the clay begins when the clay is taken from the earth. Before removing the clay, the potter prays and asks *Nung-ochu-quijo* (Earth Clay Old Lady) to be considerate of the needs of her family. "Just as you will eat us, you will feed us and clothe us, so please do not hide."

— Tessie Naranjo, Santa Clara Pueblo

Wingate black-on-red bowl, ca. 1050-1200.

W*e Navajo have stories about the sacredness of water.* 'Asdzáá Nádleehí gave our clan ancestors gish (canes). They used *gish* to strike water three times, drawing bitter, muddy, and clear water with each strike of a cane. We now have the Bitter Water, Muddy Water, and Clear Water clans. Water is very important. My family lives by *Tooh* (the San Juan River), where, like the earliest farmers, we still grow melons and corn. At eighty-four, my father still irrigates. My mother says, "He is the only one I know who can guide water up slopes. It's because he loves water."

— Gloria Emerson, Diné

Legends say that Salt Woman lived near one of the Zuni villages in ancient times. The people did not appreciate her. They polluted her home, so, she moved south, where she makes her home today near Fence Lake. Plants will not grow along the path where she walked to her new home. This may be part of an early salt-gathering trail system that originated in the San Juan Basin (Chaco Canyon) and led to the salt lake. Salt gathering was an annual male religious pilgrimage. All tribes were allowed to gather salt in peace. It was one of those unwritten laws of protection observed by all tribes.

— Edmund J. Ladd, Zuni Pueblo

Hopi people pay respect to Salt Woman. Difficult for our ancestors to obtain, salt was either secured through trade or mining. When the Hopi found a salt deposit, the location became a highly respected religious site. Hopis today still engage in ceremonial pilgrimages to gather salt. When the men bring the salt to the village, the women ritually "accept" it from the men. Women then become the caretakers and monitor the proper use of the salt for both secular and ceremonial purposes. They also decide on the distribution of the salt within the community. We also trade for salt with the Zuni people, who gather it from the salt lake located on their reservation.

— Leigh J. Kuwanwisiwma, Hopi

Zuni Salt Lake, home of Salt Woman.

Salt is an important element of our daily lives. We Hopi use it not only for meals but also in our rituals and ceremonies, and it is a part of our medicine. As my father and his fathers before him, I go to Zuni for salt. At a time before the white man came to this land, the Hopi men would be charged with the task of traveling to Zuni, New Mexico, for salt. The journey to Zuni provided the salt needed for daily living, but it also gave many different tribes a chance to exchange ideas, pottery, basketry, clothing, language, and news. Today, I still go to Zuni for salt.

—Michael Lacapa, Apache/Hopi/Tewa

These pipes, made of reed and clay, date to Ancestral Pueblo through early historic times, indicating the longevity of tobacco use in the Native American Southwest.

This pictorial rug, ca. 1970, shows a Navajo domestic scene set in a mesa landscape. Artist unknown.

Indian tobacco, wild tobacco or coyote tobacco, is sacred. Traditionally, it was never smoked for pleasure or used as a medium of exchange. The smoke from wild tobacco plants, which grow in low, moist areas, symbolizes purity and clouds that bring rain to the land. Both leaves and flowers are collected and dried for use. The dry leaves are rolled into cornhusk cigarettes. During the winter and summer solstice blessing ceremonies, religious elders declare their respect to the gods and peace for each other by exchanging the tobacco and blowing tobacco smoke in the six directions. Our ancestors used small cone-shaped clay pipes called "cloud blowers," and these have been recovered archaeologically from early Pueblo sites in the Southwest.

—Edmund J. Ladd, Zuni Pueblo

We Navajo love our animals, so they appear in our sacred stories and in our livestock prayers. Historian Ethel Lou Yazzie says the Sun gave obsidian, turquoise, abalone, and white shell horses from the east; elk, antelope, porcupine, deer, and rabbits from the south; and plants and birds from the north.

Once, my *shiná yázhí* (aunts) worried about the sheep because they acted like deer, "jumping when ____." They hired a medicine man, who ordered ____ *oo'lii* to look for herbs. My younger, seventy-three-year-old aunt drove up some steep hills with no roads. My older aunt was afraid to look out the window. Once my aunts gathered the herbs, they returned to the corral and sang for the sheep. The animals got well.

— Gloria Emerson, Diné

My elderly aunts know stories about plants. Here is my adaptation.

Atsé Hastiin (First Man) ordered animals to take care of themselves so they sowed a variety of plants. *Chaa'* (Beaver) planted *T'iisbáí* (aspen). *Bíih* (Deer) planted *Nábiih*. *Hazéí* (Squirrels) planted *Gad* (or *Hazeitsoh*). Other squirrels planted spruce, piñon, and berry bushes. *Cha'dichíízhí Hastiin* (Old Toad Men) planted *Tsa'aa*. *Na'azísí* (Gopher) planted *Da woozh* (wild berry) and wild potatoes.

Other animals planted many plants. *Shiná Yázhí* Martha says, "Plants have families like us, mothers, fathers, children. Here are *Tsin Dine'é* (Tree People), there, *Tl'oh Dine'é* (Grass People). Plants feed, heal, give colors, so say 'thanks.' Put pollen there for them."

— Gloria Emerson, Diné

Turquoise is venerated by Native Americans for its beauty and is used as gifts for the spirits. It is also a measure of personal wealth and is valuable for trade and barter. Many generations sought turquoise from the mines at Cerrillos, New Mexico. They also went searching beyond the great river and to the south, beyond the mountains of perpetual snow near the land of little rain. Raw, uncut, unpolished stones called nodules were brought back and skilled men did the finishing work. Chips and pieces left over from bead making were carefully saved to become special gifts to the gods. Turquoise collecting trips were infrequent due to the distance and other travel hardships. It was a male religious pilgrimage.

— Edmund J. Ladd, Zuni Pueblo

Minerals are for prayer, ceremony, dry painting, cleansing wool, and dye pigments. I think every Navajo carries the four sacred minerals. It's like carrying around our own miniature sacred mountains. Daily we pray and celebrate living within the circle of the grandfather mountains. Each mountain carries precious knowledge. Each is symbolized by certain birds, insects, trees, plants, songs, and prayers. Try to remember this when you think you might want to bulldoze these mountains. Let the sacred remain.

— Gloria Emerson, Diné

Background: Turquoise from Ancestral Pueblo times: Rough chunks, chips, flakes, and pendant fragments from the Pindi Pueblo excavations (ca. 1150-1300), a drilled pendant from Unshagi (ca. 1350-1550), and cylindrical beads.

PART II: **CYCLES**

Santa Clara Corn Dance, by Pablita Velarde (Tse-Tsan), Santa Clara Pueblo, 1940.

Native life is measured not in years or decades or centuries but in the cycles of the seasons, of birth and death, of coming of age and marriage, of the ceremonial round and the subsistence activities that accompany these intervals. The measure is rhythmic and recurrent and it acknowledges the essential complementarity of opposites: past and present, youth and age, male and female. As Tessie Naranjo says, "Little focus is placed on the future. There is primarily the past, what we have done; and the present, where we are now."

From childhood through adulthood, traditional gender roles, community obligations, and ceremonial responsibilities inform daily Native life. Elements of contemporary American life inform that life as well, and a Pueblo or Apache child today occupies a world of video games and Barbie dolls that are as familiar as traditional dance costumes and cradleboards. An adult Navajo male will wear Wrangler jeans, roper boots, and a western-style shirt to a traditional "sing" conducted by a elder medicine man. An adult Tohono O'odham woman with a professional job in a downtown Tucson office building still plays the sacred female game of shinney—much like field hockey, but using as a ball a small leather pouch filled with seed. As the women bat the seed pouch with sticks they perform a sacred fertile act, a way to keep the world fruitful and to make crops grow and ensure the people's health.

MOVEMENT

Turtle-shell dance rattles from Tesuque (ca. 1900) and Jemez (ca. 1920) pueblos.

Cycles are circles that travel in straight lines. The seasons come in cycles, yet each season marks the passage of another year. We receive our names, plant, harvest, marry, dance, sing, and are buried in concert with the cycles. We have danced the corn dance for hundreds of years. I am now beyond dancing, for the knee aches and the body tires much too quickly. But some things do not appear to change. I see my children dancing in the same way that I once danced. The young men still wrinkle their noses against the swamplike smell of the mud being plastered on chilled skin. And the pleasing fragrance of fresh evergreen branches still fills the kiva. My grandfather fixed the turtle and the rattle. Still good to this day, they are now part of my son's life. And we are linked by the song, for his song is now ours. Now I am part of the singers, and that is my role. Someday, my son will no longer dance and will join the singers. And we will mark the time. All people live within cycles, and in that way we are alike. In that way, we also are different.

—Anthony Dorame, Tesuque Pueblo

Movement is life. Without movement, change, and transformation, there would be no life or death. Movement is seen everywhere. The clouds rise out of the mountains and move across the sky, forming, shifting, and disappearing. The clouds become the model for the way people need to move through life. And, certainly, movement was characteristic of the ancestors, who moved across the land like the clouds across the sky.

—Tessie Naranjo, Santa Clara Pueblo

I *belong to the Hopi Greasewood clan.* Clan history contains the religious philosophy of the culture. Today, there are approximately thirty-four Hopi clans, compared to the sixty or more that once existed. Our clan traditions tell us about a spiritual covenant between the guardian deity of the Hopi Fourth Way of life and the Hopi people. This covenant required all Hopi clans to embark on migrations to place our "footprints" on the earth. Upon return to one of the mother villages, the clans that fulfilled this obligation earned the honor of "earth stewards." Among the migration footprints are ancestral villages, burial grounds, pottery sherds, petroglyphs, pictographs, trail markers, trails and springs, agricultural areas and sacred landscapes.

— Leigh J. Kuwanwisiwma, Hopi

We *get a hint of the Twins' journeys during certain chants.* There's the story of how *'Asdząą Nádleehí* sent the clans back to Navajoland on a cosmic transit system. No buses for them! We split from the other, the *Chishi* (Chiricahua) to the south, *Naashgali Diné* (Mescaleros) to the west, and *Beehai* (Jicarilla) to the north. For a while, we farmed at *Tsénaajiin* (Cabezon Peak) before moving on. The best story comes from this *Ts'eNaajiin,* who sometimes talks about an ancestor of his who was also a medicine man. His ancestor carried a big crystal in his *jish* that guided the early people away from danger when we were somewhere in the east. The crystal guided us into the embrace of our land.

— Gloria Emerson, Diné

We are born of mother's clan.
We are children of father's clan.
We are presented to Sun Father
and named by father's sister
on the fourth day of our life.
Father's sister and mother's brother
will be there for your transition
from child to adult.
When the "end of your road you reach,"
father's clan sisters prepare you
to return to the womb of Mother Earth.
— Edmund J. Ladd, Zuni Pueblo

Top: Ancestral Pueblo sandals woven of yucca and leather, dating to between A.D. 1 and 700.
Left: Traditional Navajo wedding basket made by Sandra Black, 1983.

We Navajos are taught that movement follows the sun. When you go into a hoghan (a traditional Navajo dwelling), you enter with the sun. This changes if the *Hataalii* (medicine man) ordains another pattern. When we pray, we name the grandfather mountains in order, starting with *Dzil Sisnajiní*. And we begin with our foot, closest to *Nahasdzaan* (Earth), moving upwards to our head and the sky. We think of bipolar dynamism. Male and female. Two halves of our body, the halves of the hoghan, female and male rain, and so forth. Up is for growth, down is for rainfall. In creation stories, we think upward, from first to glittering world. And when we are praying, we think of all these directions, up and down, under, over, all around us.

— Gloria Emerson, Diné

Navajo oral traditions state that there were four original clans, including Tódi ch'íínii (Bitterwater), Kinyaa'aaníí (Towering House), Hashtl'ishnii (Mud), and Hanágháanii (Walks Around). These clans are associated with places in *Dinétah* (Navajoland). Other clans came with Puebloan peoples who joined the Navajo people because of the marauding Spaniards. The Utes, Zunis, Hopis and Spanish are represented by their own clans. Navajo people joined and intermarried with other groups as well. The Navajo tribe is currently made up of over one hundred clans. It recognizes that it is a conglomeration of many Southwestern tribes. Change is in all societies, and the Navajo people have always embraced change—and this is evident in their population.

— Lillie Lane, Diné

Time is tied to the cycles of nature. The sun rises, moves across the sky, and sets to mark a time of daily living. The sun in its larger cycle gives us seasons as its arc of movement progresses in the sky. And seasons determine community activities such as planting, harvesting and resting. This overall cycle of seasons places a focus on recurrent events such as winter, summer, and their associated activities of hunting or planting. Little focus is placed on the future. There is primarily the past, what we have done; and the present, where we are now and how we are living our lives at the moment.

— Tessie Naranjo, Santa Clara Pueblo

The beginning was mist.
The first Holy Ones talked and
sang as always.
They created light, night, and day.
They sang into place the
mountains, the rivers,
plants and animals.
They sang us into life.

— Luci Tapahonso, Diné

Some may think Navajo time notions are mythic. We believe they predicted today's acceleration of time-space. In one example, '*Asdzáá Nádleehí* (Changing Woman) creates the clan ancestors and sends them homeward. They traveled here in a blink; and upon arrival they returned to normal human time. Others say they traveled slowly from the Pacific. Time is now carved into twelve months, four seasons and seven-day weeks. *Ghąąji'* (October) is the backbone of the calendar year by virtue of being both in front of winter and in back of summer. Some organize the seasons into two main branches, *Shį* (summer) and *Hai* (winter) with four secondary seasons.

— Gloria Emerson, Diné

SUMMER

In the eyes of the Great Spirit, all life is to be honored and celebrated.

Thus, Apache People honor and celebrate womanhood

in a special ceremony called the puberty feast.

Apache women are honored because,

in the equation of life-giving, they are equal.

Echoes of happiness rang throughout the universe,

when male first met female

and life began.

It was deemed that one cannot be without the other;

Human life is impossible

without both man and woman.

An Apache girl is honored as she begins her life journey,

giving birth, nurturing mankind through childhood,

keeping sacred her vows

to honor and celebrate life in all its ways,

during all its cycles, and for all time.

—Veronica E. Velarde Tiller, Jicarilla Apache

Mildred Lewis's basket features the popular "Man in the Maze" design, Tohono O'odham, 1999.

In a ritual of passage, O'odham boys ran over one hundred miles from the desert to present-day Puerto Peñasco on the coast of the Gulf of California. They were accompanied by O'odham men, who would set up campsites for the runners. The boys would collect salt on the beach for their village. The area just south of the U.S.—Mexico border is sacred, and the old trails through the volcanic rock in the Pinacate region are still visible. I am saddened that nothing has taken the place of this transition from boyhood to manhood.

—Angelo Joaquin, Jr., Tohono O'odham

An Indian Agent wrote in his report during the 1880s, "Place the same number of Whites on a barren, sandy desert such as they (the O'odham) live on and tell them to subsist there; the probability is that in two years they would become extinct." Traditional knowledge enables us to live within this arid land. The rebirth of the tohono (desert) is signaled by the coming of the summer rains. The Tohono O'odham celebrate the rains with a feast featuring wine made from bahidaj, or saguaro cactus fruit. During this time, desert farmers plant traditional crops from the seeds developed by "those who went before."

—Angelo Joaquin, Jr., Tohono O'odham

Pueblo Bonito, Chaco Canyon.

WINTER

Of the four seasons, winter is the quietest time. It is the time when earth mother rests after having given of herself by providing food for her children and other necessities needed for human survival.

—Tessie Naranjo, Santa Clara Pueblo

New Year's Dance, by Fred Kabotie, Hopi, ca. 1920.

The Navajo people learned a long time ago that winter is the ultimate test of applied faith. Winter seems harsh, but at its heart we plant a seed of great knowledge. Knowing that winter is a time of transformation, the Navajo people retreat into the warmth of hoghans, tell stories of creation, sing songs, and utter long prayers. They also play shoe and string games. These are all activities that nourish the human spirit and allow the soul to attain staying power. When winter arrives, the elders teach the sacred knowledge to younger generations, so that we, the people, may continue. Winter allows for reflection, correction, and growth.

—Rex Lee Jim, Diné

Huerfano Mesa is the doorway to our past and to our future.
The Holy People clothed her in precious fabrics.
Thus we wear clothes of soft, warm fabric.
We wear the shiny silver of clear water.
We wear turquoise made of bright skies.
We dress as they have taught us.

— Luci Tapahonso, Diné

Largo School Pueblito in Largo Canyon, New Mexico.

Our stories are told only in the winter when the snakes sleep and the snows fall. The winter is a good time for the earth to rest and the time when our grandmas and grandpas recite the legends. Our elders become our teachers and the stories become the curriculum for learning. The stories are shared from one generation to another through the oral tradition. Our stories speak of the world around us and our relationship with animals. They speak of the creator and all who were involved in the making of the world.

— Michael Lacapa, Apache/Hopi/Tewa

From left: Hopi rasp set (dance sticks) from Old Oraibi, ca. 1920, and a pair of carved and painted dance sticks made by Guadalupe Poheva of San Juan Pueblo, 1940.

We speak
Keresan, Tanoan, Uto-Aztecan,
Athabascan, and Zunian.
English
is our second language.

—Edmund J. Ladd, Zuni Pueblo

Because there are a multitude of Native American languages, radio stations broadcasting in the native tongue have a limited audience. For example, the Zuni FM station KISH occasionally broadcasts in a mixture of English and Zuni for the enjoyment of the few Zuni speakers on a reservation with a population of about ten thousand people. In the past there were attempts by missionaries to eliminate our language and culture through the removal of young boys and girls from their homes. Several young girls and boys were shipped off to Carlyle, Pennsylvania, in the 1800s. They all died from loneliness. Now, our language is dying from loneliness.

—Edmund J. Ladd, Zuni Pueblo

Grandmother is a welcome influence on my children and me now that we have returned to Taos Pueblo. She is teaching my son how to speak Tiwa through example and repetition. For instance, each time he visits Grandma, the first thing he says to her is, "*Ca*" (mother). When we moved away from Taos Pueblo, I was very young and unaware that I would lose the opportunity to learn the traditions and language. Both my children know about Nintendo, videos, and the urban environment that I experienced. Now, with Grandmother's efforts, my children are learning about their cultural heritage through the Tiwa language.

— Paula Rivera, Taos Pueblo

We sometimes gather at Navajo Community College to study the sacredness of our language and its primordial roots. Instructor Wilson Arnolith says, "*Saad*" [language] is formed as mist with the little waters in our mouth, our tongues are rainbows, and Saad travels over the rainbows . . . ."

We're told that *Diyin Dine'é* hears us only if we speak correctly. My niece Sage asks, "Are our prayers heard if we don't say them right?" We know our language has changed over the centuries, and certain phonemes are echoes from ancestral families. Holy speech, song, thought, a perfect chant are led, it is said, by the most perfect pair.

Linguist Gary Witherspoon says, "*Sa'qh Naagháí* is said to be Male. *Bik'é Hózhó* is said to be Female. This pair is manifested in the universe as bipolar pairs — *Sa'qh Naagháí* is Thought of the Universe and inner form of Speech, *Bik'é Hózhó* is Speech of the Universe and outer form of Thought."

The invocation of "*Sa'qh Naagháí doo Bik'é Hózhó*" moves me and graces my life. *Baa nitséskeesgo shił hózhóo łeh.* In certain ceremonies, songs are still accompanied by the upside-down basket, yucca strips, rattles, and flutes. As in the old days.

— Gloria Emerson, Diné

I came home one weekend and found my family watching a Phoenix Suns' basketball game on TV with the sound turned off. Instead, they were listening to KTNN Navajo radio broadcasting the game in Navajo. We winced every time the announcer yelled, "*Jóhonaa'éí,*" a sacred name of Sunbearer. Navajo radio does its part to revitalize our language. We listen to ads selling mutton, cars, and beds, and to music and news in the Navajo language. Alvino Sandoval, of the Alamo Navajo Band near Magdalena, New Mexico, and of KABR radio, helped produce a series of tapes teaching Navajo on topics such as the months of the calendar. So our language now zips through radio crystals. Words are coined and songs are sung for future generations.

— Gloria Emerson, Diné

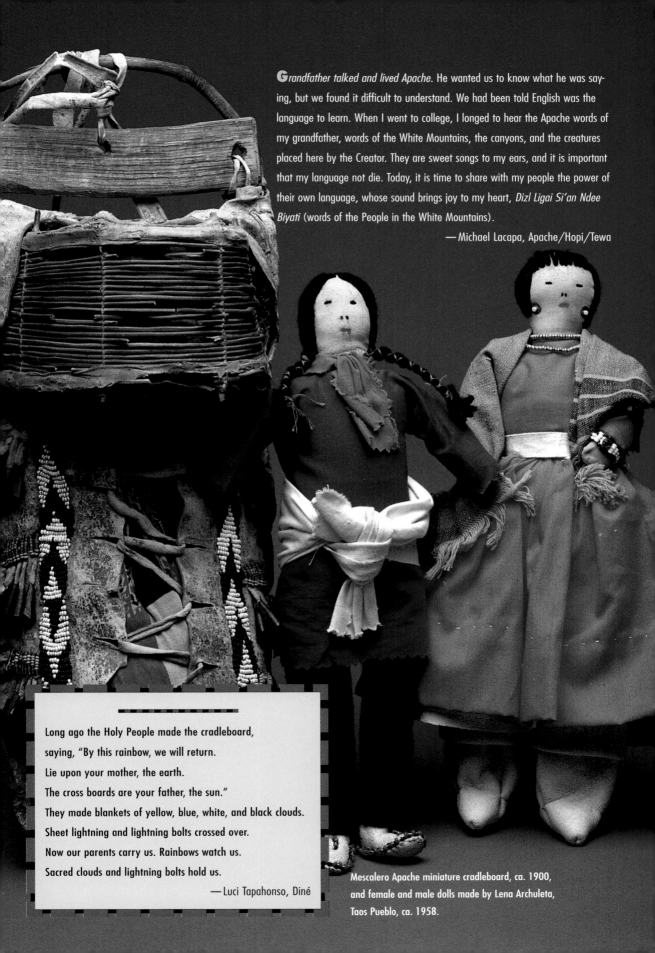

Grandfather talked and lived Apache. He wanted us to know what he was saying, but we found it difficult to understand. We had been told English was the language to learn. When I went to college, I longed to hear the Apache words of my grandfather, words of the White Mountains, the canyons, and the creatures placed here by the Creator. They are sweet songs to my ears, and it is important that my language not die. Today, it is time to share with my people the power of their own language, whose sound brings joy to my heart, *Dizl Ligai Si'an Ndee Biyati* (words of the People in the White Mountains).

—Michael Lacapa, Apache/Hopi/Tewa

Long ago the Holy People made the cradleboard,
saying, "By this rainbow, we will return.
Lie upon your mother, the earth.
The cross boards are your father, the sun."
They made blankets of yellow, blue, white, and black clouds.
Sheet lightning and lightning bolts crossed over.
Now our parents carry us. Rainbows watch us.
Sacred clouds and lightning bolts hold us.

—Luci Tapahonso, Diné

Mescalero Apache miniature cradleboard, ca. 1900,
and female and male dolls made by Lena Archuleta,
Taos Pueblo, ca. 1958.

Drummers for the Comanche Dance, San
Ildefonso Pueblo, January 1933.
Inset: Drum and beater made by Lorenzo
Herrera, Cochiti Pueblo, ca. 1920.

Pottery, dance, and all other forms of life expression continually remind us of our connections to the natural world. Pottery reminds us of the sacred earth bowl within which we live. The design work on our pots helps us to remember the mountains, clouds, lightning and plants upon whom we depend for our spiritual and physical survival. Dance is about movement, which creates energy to be shared with the clouds who bring rain for our crops. Dancing is also about remembering our connection to the clouds and the earth.

—Tessie Naranjo, Santa Clara Pueblo

When you are dancing, all the sound vibrates within you. Your body becomes one instrument among others, a part of the whole. Through this do we become joined to creation, to those who have gone before and to those who are yet to be. Our dances, songs, and prayers join us to our world. Although the drum is often the dominant sound, no one instrument stands alone. The drum, the rattle, bells, and shells create undulating levels of rhythm. The chorus of voices blends with all these elements to make a song to heaven.

—Tony Chavarria, Santa Clara Pueblo

Left: Flute player, Hopi Arizona ca. 1911.
Photo by H.F. Robinson MNM Neg. No. 21621
This page from left: Taos flute of painted cane
and buckskin, ca. 1900; Tohono O'odham (Pima)
flute of painted cane with cut designs and finger holes,
ca. 1920; carved cedar flute made by Phillip Haozous,
Chiricahua Apache, 1977.

As a novice Hopi composer, I am consistently reminded that the words of a song are a humble petition to the spiritual forces for their blessings. My father and grandfather taught me that my corn plants are my children. By singing to the corn, I help them to mature. Indeed, the best place to contemplate and compose a song is in the solitude of my cornfield. The women would sing grinding songs to the rhythm of the metate and mano as they ground the corn into flour. Our traditions say that the stones become happy and honored when they hear the grinding songs.

— Leigh J. Kuwanwisiwma, Hopi

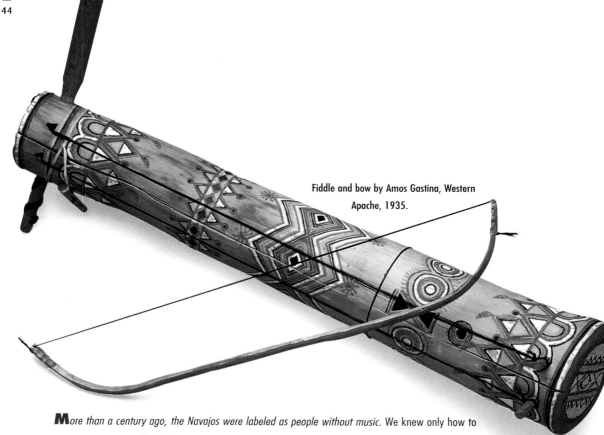

Fiddle and bow by Amos Gastina, Western Apache, 1935.

More than a century ago, the Navajos were labeled as people without music. We knew only how to grunt. In contrast to that fallacy, today the reservation resounds with song and dance or powwow competitions or benefits where Navajos of all ages display their musical and dancing abilities. The Navajo Arts and Humanities Council and Navajo Community College sponsor a Native American Music Festival. There Navajo musicians such as Vincent Craig, Bahe Billy, Rex Redhair, and bands like Aces Wild and Burning Sky jam with modern instruments and successfully integrate traditional and contemporary music. Although, traditionally, Navajos used musical instruments like the water drum, the ceremonial flute, and the basket, today's generation celebrates life with a variety of instrument, song, and music.

—Rex Lee Jim, Diné

Navajos believe babies are born with intellectual, emotional, and spiritual capabilities. Babies usually laugh for the first time at three months. It is best for a baby to laugh to a relative who is good-natured. The person who makes a baby laugh for the first time has to host a party to celebrate the baby's successful transition into the adult world. This person provides food, treats, and natural salt. Salt is an additional transition marker. Relatives and friends come to the baby's "first laugh party" to assure there will always be togetherness. The honored baby and family serve food from a Navajo basket with a pinch of natural salt. As guests accept their food, they pray for happiness and generosity.

—Lillie Lane, Diné

PART III: COMMUNITY

Hopi Family, by Otis Polelonema, Hopi, 1948.

The village or community is the human dwelling or living place. It is where the people meet the needs of survival and where they weave their web of connections. Native communities are about connections because relationships form the whole. Each individual becomes part of the whole community, which includes the hills, mountains, rocks, trees, and clouds.

—Tessie Naranjo, Santa Clara Pueblo

Laguna Pueblo dwelling, ca. 1915.

If the earth is the origin and source of creation for Native peoples of the Southwest, home and community are the heartbeat. From the open hearth in a teepee to the all-electric kitchen in a modern home, community begins in this center place of family warmth, sharing, and connection—a connection that extends outward through the community and into the surrounding landscape following ties of kinship, of ceremony, of work and subsistence, of artistic creation, and of trade.

Outside the home, community connections include the plants and animals with which Native lives are intertwined, and the voices in this section tell stories of seeds and harvests, herding and hunting, cooking and sharing. Utilitarian items such as digging sticks and iron hoes take on sacred meaning when they are used to grow the life-giving corn, and religious items such as stone hunting fetishes serve a quotidian function when they assist the hunter in finding the animal that will give him the gift of his life.

Throughout the Southwest, the materials of daily life have always been both gathered locally and exchanged over great distances. Just as today's Pueblo home may hold a television set made in Japan, a kiva in Chaco Canyon a thousand years ago might have housed a brilliant red parrot carried overland from deep in Central America. At the center of trade and exchange today are the art works created by Native peoples. Bought, sold, and prized around the world, contemporary Indian pottery, textiles, baskets, and silverwork continue to speak eloquently of the beauty and struggle that have characterized the lives of the people who inhabit this sacred land.

> Made of stone and mud, the foundation, the four corners.
> Made of earth and wood, the roof, the center.
> All anchored with prayers.
>
> —Edmund J. Ladd, Zuni Pueblo

HOME

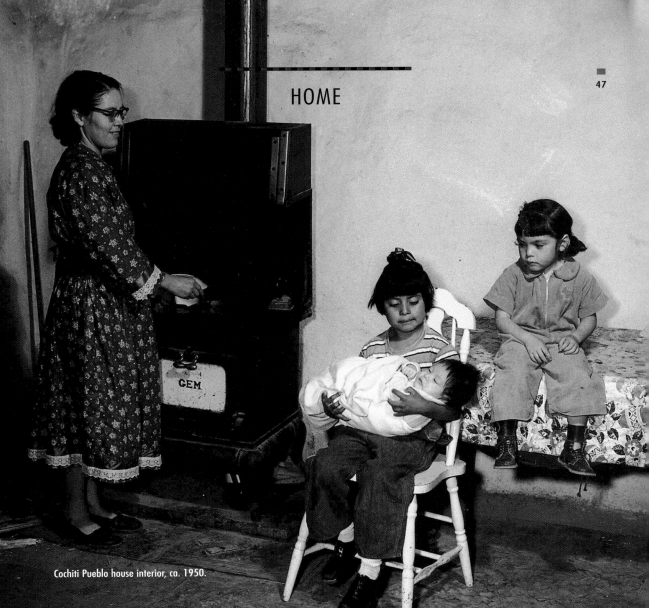

Cochiti Pueblo house interior, ca. 1950.

We Pueblo people hold healing ceremonies for our homes, just as we do for any member of the community. Our structures are extensions of our world order and are viewed as living beings with life and death cycles. Shelter is not just a place to live but an extension of the natural world and the sacred realm. The house reflects the relationship of earth and sky, mother and father. Houses are also symbols of the larger ordering of the universe in which mountains, hills and valleys define spaces where humans can dwell. Building and creating shelter brings the human and the cosmic forms together. The roof or ceiling of the structure may be seen as the sky, or the father, which protects and nurtures the people who live inside. The floor is the Mother Earth, which embraces us when we die.

Stone, adobe, and reed and wood *vigas,* or poles, were once the primary materials of construction in the Southwest. These readily available natural materials were not heavily processed. Stone was minimally cut. Adobe was shaped by hand. The human hand was the primary tool for creation. Our construction techniques have changed, and not all our homes are adobe anymore. When my father built my house, he chose frame construction. It is a six-hundred-square-foot building, a home that is very small by today's standards but would have been large by my ancestors' standards.

—Tessie Naranjo, Santa Clara Pueblo

The Pueblo kitchen was the gathering place of the extended family. The great-grandmother, grandmother, or mother would be in the kitchen preparing and cooking food. In the late 1800s, the Pueblo kitchen might have included a table, chairs or benches, wooden cupboards, clay storage jars of grains, baskets of ground corn, and a fireplace or wood-stove. Generally there was also an outdoor *horno* (clay oven) near the kitchen. In the 1990s, the woodstove might have been replaced by a gas or electric stove, and refrigerators and freezers added. The clay storage jars may be gone, and ground corn no longer kept in a basket but the kitchen still remains the central place of the home.

—Tessie Naranjo, Santa Clara Pueblo

There have never been electricity or plumbing at my grandmother's house. In her kitchen, she has two stoves: a 1950s propane stove and a 1920s woodstove. The contrast between "new" and "old" is striking, and the two stoves are reminders of the memories and experiences that have occurred there. The kitchen is the main gathering place for our families. There is always an abundance of conversation and laughter around the table. In my house, there are "modern" conveniences, but the family gatherings, the laughter and memories still take place in the kitchen.

—Paula Rivera, Taos Pueblo

Many pictures come to mind when I think of the heart of our home, my grandmother's kitchen. The large Zia pot sitting in the corner stored the bread. Only the women were allowed to get the bread from inside, and I felt special when asked to do this. Many baskets hung on the walls. We filled these baskets, often to put bread on the table, to take food to the dancers, or to pay a hunter for a fine rabbit. As we sat around the big round table, we told the day's events and shared much laughter. Our table never ran out of food, no matter how many of us there were. There was always enough for any guests, and there always seemed to be guests.

—Carlotta Penny Bird, Santo Domingo Pueblo

Apache camp, New Mexico, ca. 1905.

The teepee suited the lifestyle of Indians on the move. Poles and skins were easily obtained, constructed and transported. The teepee provided all the comforts of home. Around the teepee fire, stories and traditions, prayers and songs, philosophies and customs were passed from generation to generation. That is why the teepee is an enduring and permanent structure in Apache and Ute societies. Moreover, the teepee reflected the deep respect that Indians have for their horses. It was the horse that transported the teepee over mountains, through valleys and grasslands, following the buffalo and other game. The burden could not be too great for this beautiful and sacred animal.

—Veronica E. Velarde Tiller, Jicarilla Apache

> The round-roof hooghan is like a woman's tier skirt.
> It is said that the mother, *amá*, is the heart of the home.
> It is said that there is beauty within
> when a home is as it should be.
> Beauty extends from the *hooghan*.
> Beauty extends from the woman.
>
> — Luci Tapahonso, Diné

*I*n Navajo, *hooghan* means home. A *hooghan* is a circular, one-room structure that always faces the east to catch first light. Traditionally, a hooghan was made of cedar logs with bark and mud on the exterior. A *hooghan* can be home for a family, but it also can be transformed into a sacred structure for intricate healing ceremonies. Upon death, a person can be put to rest in a hooghan, in which case it should not be disturbed. A *hooghan* is a microcosm of Navajo philosophy. Navajo people believe they live in the bosom of Mother Earth.

Navajo oral traditions say that the Holy People lived on earth before the "earth surface people." The Holy People dictated that Diné should live in round homes called *hooghan nímazí*. Today, *hooghan nímazí* are round or octagonal and can be made of any building material available. Throughout Navajoland, there are traditional *hooghans*, rock *hooghans*, and combinations of lumber, rock, and earth *hooghans*. There are even solar *hooghans*, two-story *hooghans* and hooghans with bathroom additions. The earth *hooghans* have evolved as Navajo people modernized. Although today there is a lot of outside influence, Navajos still need *hooghans* for healing ceremonies. The Holy People recognize only the *hooghan*.

— Lillie Lane, Diné

*T*ools and materials for building were always simple and taken from nature. For example, a shelter could be built from rabbitbrush to provide shade during the heat of the summer. For building more permanent structures, shaped stones had many uses, including digging, shaping, and pounding. Pueblo builders polished floors and walls with round cobblestones and pottery sherds. These tools were used as an extension of the human hand. The types of tools we use now have changed. Like everyone else, we have become familiar with hoes, shovels, nails, and trowels.

— Tessie Naranjo, Santa Clara Pueblo

Apache wickiups, early twentieth century.

Our Hopi ancestors developed building techniques to create shelter and relief from the severe cold and blistering heat. The use of stone and mortar was not only practical but was ultimately required by tradition. Although men were primarily responsible for construction, the women, who maintained the structures, decided the layout. Hence, building was a cooperative effort.

—Leigh J. Kuwanwisiwma, Hopi

Imagine an island of shade in the sea of sunlight flooding the desert! Built with mesquite posts, saguaro ribs, and greasewood from the desert, the ramada provides a cool, dry place to work and to enjoy meals. It is a storage place and can be used to dry meat (jerky). Foods can hang safely from the eaves in baskets woven from baling wire. My mother or my grandmother gently coaxed many a child to sleep in a swing suspended from the supports. We older children would sometimes compete to see who could swing the child the highest—until the swing would bang against the ramada and frighten the poor baby and us.

—Angelo Joaquin, Jr., Tohono O'odham

Housing and Urban Development (HUD) housing developments are not a mark of progress for the O'odham. Traditionally, families lived in clustered units with parents' homes surrounded by the houses of their children. Relatives lived next door, ready to help at a moment's notice. Children were disciplined by all the elders. Today, in HUD-constructed subdivisions, the people living next door may not even speak the same dialect, are most likely not related and have no stake in the upbringing of children other than their own. This is contributing to the increase in social problems, including gangs and substance abuse. As Indian people, we must assess progress by looking at the impact on our society.

—Angelo Joaquin, Jr., Tohono O'odham

Women replastering a house in Paguate Village, Laguna Pueblo, 1925.

AGRICULTURE

Manos and metates, used for grinding.

Born of Mother Earth, we originated with good and evil. The witch hid in the darkness of the Fourth World. Because he carried death, the elders denied him entry into the new world. The witch said, "When you find the center place, and you increase, and there is no means to reduce your numbers, you will starve. To solve this, I bring death, but I also bring life. Blue corn for life and white corn for the gods." When the people found the center place, they planted the seeds in the flesh of Mother Earth, where they reproduced and multiplied.

—Edmund J. Ladd, Zuni Pueblo

Agriculture as practiced by the Zuni was very simple and labor intensive but effective. A good pair of hands, a strong back, and a sturdy planting stick were the essentials. They made a "wooden leg," which was a stiltlike tool, from a juniper limb with a branch left on the side and used it as a lever for pushing down into the wet soil. Later a stone hoe and still later a metal hoe brought in by the Indian trader became indispensable for planting corn, beans, and squash.

—Edmund J. Ladd, Zuni Pueblo

There is a season for harvest,
a season for growth,
a season for tending,
a season for caring,
a time for planting,
a time for resting,
a time for enjoyment.

—Edmund J. Ladd, Zuni Pueblo

Our old stories are important links to our past. Here are two of many stories of early farming:

First Man and First Woman gave white and yellow corn. *T'azhii* (Turkey) danced around, shaking forth red, black, blue, and gray corn kernels. *Tlúsh-Tsoh* (Big Snake) gave pumpkin, watermelon, cantaloupe and muskmelon seeds. This story comes from historian Ethel Lou Yazzie.

The other story comes from my mother. Her uncle planted a garden. On moonlit nights, the children helped him haul water in *tsintóshjeeh* (wooden barrels). Each child carried water in buckets with wire handles. My mother remembers how on certain nights, they carried water to plants and played in the moonlight. This might have been in the 1920s.

— Gloria Emerson, Diné

Who remembers the luscious juiciness of a watermelon just severed from its stem? The sweetness of fresh corn from the stalk? Who washed winnowed wheat in a yucca basket? We could not remember, and the younger people did not know. For years, wheat fields and cornfields were idle. We blamed the economy and forgot to farm. But someone did remember. Leaders intervened, and the people cooperated and lent their landholdings. We purchased farm equipment to share and elected to ban chemicals. Chile plants prospered alongside fields of coriander, and the elders cried from happiness. Today, we again hear the musical thump of a watermelon being split open in the field. Will we forget again what we now remember?

— Anthony Dorame, Tesuque Pueblo

Since I am from a family of traditional farmers and shepherds, I am emotionally bonded to the land and the animals. We are taught that we are at the mercy of nature. Treat the earth and environment with respect, humility, and cooperatively and it will in turn provide for you. Our life is corn, and we still practice farming without irrigation. I believe that Hopi corn is among the most drought-resistant seed stock still left in the world. Perhaps the Hopi prophecy that our way of life and our corn will someday save the world will come true.

—Leigh J. Kuwanwisiwma, Hopi

To farm successfully, a farmer has to be a soil scientist, a botanist, a hydrologist, and much more. For hundreds of years, indigenous farmers planted many varieties of crops, built extensive irrigation systems, and stored and traded their surplus. Nonetheless, they were careful not to exhaust the soil, erode the lands, or deprive wildlife of their ranges and habitats. Raising livestock or ranching has been a recent (mid-1800s) phenomenon among Indian tribes. Indian people quickly adapted to ranching, since working with animals in wide-open spaces was natural. Sheep raising among the Navajo became an economic mainstay, and cattle ranching remains a viable part of the Apache tribal economies today.

—Veronica E. Velarde Tiller, Jicarilla Apache

Hornos, traditional outdoor ovens, at Laguna Pueblo, ca. 1940.

Before our feast day each summer, the ovens must be prepared. They must be replastered with a new coat of adobe mud. Helping my grandmother replaster the oven taught me an understanding of the proper order of things. One of the uncles would always say, "We should plaster it with cement so you won't have to work so hard." But this never happened; perhaps the oven was necessary for our own renewal. One can tell the seasons by the use of the oven. Important events bring the women together to help each other make the bread and prepare meals to sustain the community. As children we played nearby because the first loaf out of the oven would be for us.

—Carlotta Penny Bird, Santo Domingo Pueblo

An elderly weaver, during an interview, patiently "wove" the cord of the small microphone pinned to her lapel into a single strand as she spoke respectfully of the Himdag, or "Way of Life." The O'odham Himdag teaches us that plants, animals, and humans are equal and all must be treated with respect. The act of harvesting yucca, beargrass, banana yucca root, and devil's claw allows humans to walk among the other members of the community. O'odhams offer a prayer of thanks and contrition to the plant for giving of itself.

—Angelo Joaquin, Jr., Tohono O'odham

Luck plays a large part in the success of the hunt. Today, hunting is not necessary for survival, but it was to our ancestors. They carefully planned the harvest. Out of respect, the people prayed and made offerings to the animals. In some cases, such as the rabbit hunts, women, both young and old, participated and contributed. After a successful hunt, the community cooperated to process the carcass. Nothing was wasted. They used the hides for clothing and shelter and the bones for tools such as awls. They consumed some of the meat and preserved some as "dry meat" for long-term storage. Today, we still continue the practice of ceremonial hunts and pay religious homage to the spirit of the animal to increase our luck.

—Leigh J. Kuwanwisiwma, Hopi

Zuni hunting fetishes from the about the turn of the century.

Hunting means, ultimately, converting animal energy into human energy. Respect for this power demands that Navajo hunters cleanse themselves physically and spiritually in the sweathouse. They ask Talking God and Black God for the most tasty meat from their supply. The hunters then ask to make proper use of their weapons, the dark bow with the tail-feathered arrow and the feathered bow with the second tail-feathered arrow. During the hunt, they use an ancient language of prayer to communicate and contemplate only holy thoughts. The hunters take only what they need. At the site of the kill, they pray and sing and ask for all the blessings of the Deer People. At home they eat all the meat and return the bones to sacred places.

—Rex Lee Jim, Diné

My hunting stick is not a tool of death but a tool of life. I throw it like the boomerang it resembles. When my father gave it to me, he said it could make me a great hunter and help me bring food home. It would help feed my grandmother when Grandpa could no longer hunt. How simple this hunting tool is! It amazes me that my ancestors could conceive such a perfect but simple tool.

— Michael Lacapa, Apache/Hopi/Tewa

By listening to the elders, we learned a "low-tech" way to catch rabbits. We inserted a long, sharp, pointed stick in a rabbit hole and twirled the stick rapidly. The rabbit's skin became entangled in the stick, and we would pull out the bunny like a fish on a line. We were deadly with homemade slingshots and hunted birds for food and ceremonies. Red rubber for slingshots came from discarded inner tubes. This rubber was not synthetic, and we prized its ability to stretch. Then Grandfather gave me a shotgun. Pounded by the recoil, I would come home with a bloody lip and a handful of doves. A .22 rifle was next. With our new weaponry, we had become hunters, or so we thought.

— Anthony Dorame, Tesuque Pueblo

Hunting is men's work. Some still have their own prayers, songs, and rituals. The rituals now include modern conveniences. The *tséníł yázhí* (hatchet or tomahawk) has been replaced by the steel hatchet. The bowguard and bow and arrows are replaced by rifles. Navajo women still stay at home and pray.

— Gloria Emerson, Diné

Hopi rabbit hunting stick, ca. 1890.

ARTS

Each vase wears a necklace of prayer and song.
"Come inside," we beseech the pottery, "teach us the song
that brings joy to cooking. Teach us to pray
that we may be generous and humble."
Our pottery teaches the sacred sounds of cooking.

— Luci Tapahonso, Diné

Storage jar by María and Julian Martínez,
San Ildefonso Pueblo, 1938-1939.

An early polychrome olla by María and Julian Martínez, San Ildefonso Pueblo, 1917.

My grandparents are artists as defined by Western culture; one is a silversmith, and the other is a painter. They are also artists when they plow their fields, tend to their horses, and grind their corn. I am also an artist when I make a basket to take to the *kiva* or bake bread in the *horno* in preparation for a feast day. To me, "art" is my children, my work, my home, and my community.

— Paula Rivera, Taos Pueblo

The earliest stories I know about "art" come from *'Asdzą́ą́ Na'ashje"ii* (Spider Woman) and *'Asdzą́ą́ Nádleehí* (Changing Woman). Spider Woman taught her grandchildren and *Nayeel Ashkii* (Boy Dreamer) how to make pictures with string. Changing Woman ordained the *Hashtł'ishnii* (Mud) Clan to become creative people. This connection between mud and creativity first appears in the clan origin stories. Although people say there's no word for art in the Navajo language, we do have names for image making. Those who follow the Beauty Way watch sandpaintings emerge on sand altars, and we know the Holy People endowed *'ii kááh* (dry paintings) with healing. Their gifts are enacted in curative dramas like Nightway Chant. Also, *Na'ach'ąąh* means making art. *Na'ach'ąąhi'í* is maker of art. Our early families were contemplative artists who bound rainbow and lightning into looms, and sunbeam and mountains into baskets. This is our artistic inheritance. Like holiness flowing through plants, art and the *Diné bee'íínáájí* (Navajo Way) are continually energized. Things called "art" were originally made to invoke spiritual powers and to return the sick to harmony. So if art was the invocation of beauty, then *Diné 'iináájí* was and is art.

— Gloria Emerson, Diné

Hopi basket with kachina design, 1930.

The word "art" is not found in our language. But what do we call a piece of work created by the hands of my family? What will we call that piece which embodies the life of its creator? What will it be if it has a life and soul, while its maker sings and prays for it? In my home we call it pottery, painted with designs to tell us a story. In my mother's house, we call it a wedding basket to hold blue cornmeal for the groom's family. In my grandma's place, we call it a kachina doll, a carved image of a life force that holds the Hopi world in place. We make pieces of life to see, touch, and feel. Shall we call it "art"? I hope not. It may lose its soul. It is life. It is people.

— Michael Lacapa,
Apache/Hopi/Tewa

What is now called "art" Native people first made for utility. This includes containers for food and paints and cooking vessels. Every woman, man, and child was an "artist." For example, if a cooking vessel broke, one had to make a new one because there were no stores with replacements. Then the middleman, the Indian trader, arrived with his cheap aluminum cookware, which soon replaced the handmade wares. He saw the value of Indian art and helped to develop the Indian "artist." The Indian person quickly discovered that he could make a clay pot, paint designs on it, and get some of the trade goods. Tin and aluminum do not break so easily.

— Edmund J. Ladd, Zuni Pueblo

WEAVING

Classic Period
Navajo serape,
ca. 1840–1869.

I bought an old *ts'aa'* (basket) at the flea market. My mother held it to the afternoon sun to show its tight weave. "You'll use it for a long time," she said. We looked at jewelry, exquisite rugs, pottery, fine velvet clothes. We lingered, musing over details. Nearby was what we craved—snowcones. The sugary ice melted quickly. Then we saw the Avon Lady and got serious.

—Luci Tapahonso, Diné

One day, a young Diné woman fell into Spider couple's busy underground den. Every day she watched Na'ashjé'ii Asdząąn (Spider Woman) spin and spin, while Na'ashjé'ii Hastiin (Spider Man) helped gather materials. After spinning enough fiber, the spider couple searched for a place to weave their rugs. The young woman saw their hard work. She learned to spin, and Na'ashjé'ii Asdząąn helped her put up a loom. They worked together daily. After the young woman learned the entire weaving process, the Spider couple made her return to her people. Navajos teach children that spiders are their grandparents. Navajo weavers always deliberately put a mistake in their rugs so their creativity will continue into every rug.

—Lillie Lane, Diné

Embroidered shirt by Ramoncita Sandoval, San Juan Pueblo, 1992.

Pueblo people used looms made from tree limbs and tools such as wooden shuttles and combs to make their own clothing. Wintertime was the usual time for weaving cloth to be sewn into clothes. Bone awls and needles were used to stitch leather and cotton cloth. Shoes were woven from yucca or stitched from leather. We no longer use the looms for making our everyday clothing. As a child, I remember wearing mostly hand-me-down clothes sent to my family by Protestant churches from neighboring states such as Texas and Oklahoma. Now, I mostly wear store-bought clothes.

—Tessie Naranjo, Santa Clara Pueblo

Hopi manta, ca. 1930, cotton and wool.

A mong the Hopi, men are the weavers. Traditionally, most of the weaving occurs in a kiva, an underground ceremonial house. Weaving in this setting enables the men to socialize and teach traditions and rituals to the younger men and boys. Today, the Hopi are one of the suppliers of ceremonial textiles to other Pueblos. Individuals specialize in different types of textiles and garments. Hopi men and women who die are buried in ceremonial garments and blankets. Our designs tell stories, teach history and religious philosophy, and are aesthetically pleasing.

—Leigh J. Kuwanwisiwma, Hopi

CONTAINERS

Clockwise lower left: Wooden ladle from Hopi, ca. 1910; Hopi mountain sheep horn ladle, ca. 1920; wooden ladle from San Felipe Pueblo, 1880.

I n the Pueblo world, containers were made from clay and brush. Clay pots not only held food but were used for eating, drinking, and for ceremonies. Baskets of all sizes and shapes were made from brush and grasses that grow in and around any village. Gourds were used to hold and carry water or as ladles for drinking. Today, the containers found in our households have changed. The same plastic and metal containers found anywhere in the country are now in every Pueblo household.

— Tessie Naranjo, Santa Clara Pueblo

P ots made from clay were the major cooking utensils and were used for cooking beans, a staple of Pueblo people. Long spoons made from clay, as well as long wooden sticks, were kept handy for stirring the beans. Long, thin, flat stones heated over a fire were used to make a waferlike bread called *piki* bread. Other small stones were used to help boil stews. Flint knives were used to cut meat and for drying and cooking. Now it is rare to see a Pueblo mother using a clay pot to cook beans for her family. One of my special childhood memories is that moment when I opened the door to our home and smelled stew or beans cooking in a clay bean pot.

— Tessie Naranjo, Santa Clara Pueblo

Santa Clara storage jar, ca. 1900.

Canteens intrigue me. They have a simple purpose but many stories. Maybe it's the relationship between earth and water or the concept of a vessel and how we ourselves are vessels. Maybe I relate because I am big and bulky too. I realize how heavy they are when filled with water. The weight of the big, bulky canteen compares to the weight of the two plastic bottles of water I carried in my backpack while tromping through the jungles of Mexico.

— Tony Chavarria, Santa Clara Pueblo

Shádí (Aunt) Bertha said the earliest Navajo made a pot but could not figure out how to fire it. They tried many methods with no success. Finally 'Asdzą́ą́ Na'ashjé'ii (Spider Woman) said, "Give it to me, I'll get it fired." So she took it to the Sun, who fired it.

— Gloria Emerson, Diné

TRADE

Untitled painting by Navajo artist Gerald Nailor, 1937.

If *American Indian trade activity could have been measured prior to 1492, it would have been the equivalent of commercial activity throughout the world.* In the Southwest, the indigenous peoples had an extensive trade network up and down the Rio Grande Valley, into the Rocky Mountains, and into the Eastern Plains. Contrary to stereotyped views, exchange did not consist solely of Apaches, Navajos, and Utes raiding the Pueblos for their crops. Hunters exchanged meat, hides, leather goods, natural foods and, later, horses for the great variety of crops of the Rio Grande farmers. A multitude of medicinal plants and religious paraphernalia were bartered. Artisans bought and sold household items, pottery, baskets, and decorative materials. Commerce encouraged cultural exchange, intermarriage, the sharing of knowledge, ceremonies, languages, and the growth of respect and understanding for other tribes' territories, religions, and customs. Often warfare resulted, but it never led tribes to raise standing armies. It was upon this aboriginal trade network that the Europeans established the foundation for conquest. They simply introduced new goods using unfair means, including liquor, bribes, and the bayonet, to gain economic, social, and political power over Indian people.

—Veronica E. Velarde Tiller, Jicarilla Apache

My grandmother went from Taos Pueblo to Zuni Pueblo to learn how to make jewelry. She won a blue ribbon for a squash blossom necklace with Zuni Shalako kachinas, and her unique style contributed to the growth of the Native American industry of silversmithing. We traveled long distances from Taos Pueblo to southern Colorado to Arizona to sell to many different shops and galleries. Grandma's jewelry, now worn by many people, has touched numerous lives.

— Paula Rivera, Taos Pueblo

Hand-shaped pendant necklace of inlaid shell, Santa Domingo Pueblo, ca. 1890.

Our family went visiting at Red Rock and Oaksprings. We played on auntie's smooth dirt floor while the grownups talked.

Outside, heat waves shimmered above shrubs and piñon trees.

Later, at the trading post, we saw "our old father," Daddy's older brother. We were surprised and shy.

Our footsteps echoed in the dim store as we headed for the freezer.

"Our old father" bought us orange Dreamsicles.

We sat in the pickup bed, licking the cold sweetness. He smiled, saying, "This tastes really good."

We were happy about him.

— Luci Tapahonso, Diné

Anthropologists classifying the Pueblos as sedentary people do not grasp the larger picture. Our home is filled with evidence of a long-standing tradition of travel, trade, and learning. We use pottery of our own, as well as pottery from neighboring villages and from as far away as Acoma, Zuni, and Hopi. My grandfather's favorite bolo tie to wear on special occasions was one made in Zuni depicting a Shalako. Our living room is draped with Navajo rugs on the floor, chairs, and walls. A Victrola and television are modern additions. Stories about travel and new friends come down through time. In the past, travel took many days, so the visits were longer and resulted in the sharing of songs, ceremonies, and languages. Elders who never attended school spoke Spanish and several Native languages very well.

— Carlotta Penny Bird, Santo Domingo Pueblo

Trading posts were remote outposts that supplied food, clothing, tools, and other practical items for the Navajo home. Initially, Navajo men traded rugs, baskets, and jewelry for supplies, since the only transportation was the horse. Over time, trading posts flourished as Navajo livestock owners began selling wool and lambs annually. Many Navajo people were given credit accounts that allowed them to buy necessities at any time. Some families were able to purchase wagons, manual appliances, and vehicles with their profits. Trading posts were bustling businesses for remote Navajo families and communities. Today, there are few trading posts.

— Lillie Lane, Diné

Rez Ball, photograph by Monty Roessel, 1990s.

Nearly fifty years ago, I heard a professor predict that in a few years Pueblo culture would be gone. A cash economy was replacing the agricultural foundation of the Pueblos. Veterans returning from World War II were highly unlikely to resume their prewar lifeways. The federal policies of relocation and termination of trust responsibility were certain to bring traditional life to a close.

This analysis was scholarly and logical, but it was wrong. You will understand what I mean when visiting any of the hundred of ancient communities, carefully laid out in the canyons and on the plateaus of the surrounding mountains. There along the cliff faces, the steps you take and the places you use to steady yourself are the footprints and handholds worn

PART IV: **SURVIVAL**

into the soft tufa stone by countless generations of our ancestors.

Like the marks left in ageless stones, tradition is deeply etched into our very being. The past awakens in the present through ceremonies received long ago in these plateau places. Generations of families gathered here; we are of these spaces, places, and times. We leave our footprints for another generation; we

We are of the earth.

We emerged from the earth.

We replenish the earth.

We grow old.

We return to the earth.

—Edmund J. Ladd, Zuni Pueblo

Dinosaur jar by Andrew Pacheco,
Santo Domingo Pueblo, 1991.

My people, the Zuni, settled along the banks of the stream now known as the "Zuni River." Our grandfathers spoke of other people with whom they were in contact through their trade network. They also spoke of a prophecy that said, "Beware! In time they will return, those who were pushed beyond our lands. They will come drinking 'black water,' speaking nonsense, making pictures with a stick, and they will claim this land as theirs. They will come like thunder in the sky. They will turn brother against brother. When this happens the world will soon be turned upside down."

The prophecy is coming true. In 1539, the Moor Estevanico came to our village, and we killed him as a "slave spy." On July 7, 1540, Don Francisco Vásquez de Coronado came and disrupted the solstice ceremonies and did battle with our grandfathers. The missionaries came next. All who came claimed this land as theirs. In my opinion, the coffee-drinking, foul-talking people who make thunder in the sky with their jet aircraft are the people of the prophecy. Despite these impacts, our culture survives.

— Edmund J. Ladd, Zuni Pueblo

Dios (the Spanish god) and the spokesperson of our spiritual deities met east of our village. They talked a long time, then decided to have a contest to see whose ways were stronger. They first made food. Our cornmeal lasted much longer in the stomach than their flour tortillas. Next the contestants sang and danced. Our dances brought the rain to the fields, and their bailes (social dances) left them weakened and hung over. As each contest was waged, the Spanish people saw that our ways were strong and to survive they would have to learn from us. Spanish people who have long lived near us share our ways. The greatest compliment to give them is to say, "You are generous of heart and know how to share your food."

— Carlotta Penny Bird, Santo Domingo Pueblo

By the time the Americans arrived in the Southwest in the mid-1840s, the Spanish had been here for three hundred years. American traders took away resources, such as turquoise, piñon nuts, seeds, and animal skins. By the end of the 1800s, archaeologists and photographers had gone into every Pueblo village. They were curious about our past. About the same time, the United States government forced changes in our religion and education. Boarding schools removed children from their homes and communities. Despite these attempts, Southwest tribal cultures have survived. As survivors, we use those nontraditional ways that we wish and keep out those that we don't like. Like all modern people, we Pueblos have been shaped by our history. Often, I feel uncomfortable with the necessity of conforming to Western cultural standards. Whenever I feel the need to retreat, the safety and comfort of my community is where I go to find myself again.

—Tessie Naranjo, Santa Clara Pueblo

After the Long Walk in the 1860s, federal government agents wrenched children from frenzied parents and herded these unfortunate youngsters into stark schools. My mother remembers how they arrived at the school with their shawls and Navajo clothes. One little girl named Mabel wouldn't release her shawl when the school people tried to pull it from her. She screamed as she was dragged around grasping her shawl. My mother says she and others cried so Mabel could keep her shawl. Our next federal-sponsored migration occurred in the 1950s when Navajos were relocated by the hundreds to Chicago, Seattle, and Los Angeles. When relocation ended, many returned home, thankful that Congress's forced migration plan had ended and that we had become forgotten targets.

—Gloria Emerson, Diné

The coming of "non-Indian foreigners" brought both good and bad. The Hopi suffered more during the period of dominance and suppression of the Spanish era. The Spanish introduced metal tools to the Native people, enabling them to do more in agriculture, building, and hunting. Many Spanish terms are incorporated into Hopi vocabulary. In 1680, the Hopi participated in the Great Pueblo Revolt and helped drive the Spanish from the area. We were never reconquered. Later, we experienced the western Anglo intrusions as the government forced Hopi children into boarding schools to "civilize" them. Christians also attempted their form of assimilation. Today, we proudly claim to be a non-Christian community with a culture that is among the strongest of all Native Americans in North America.

—Leigh J. Kuwanwisiwma, Hopi

Jicarilla Apache basketry water bottle, ca. 1910.

General Kearny's entry into New Mexico in 1846 brought decades of warfare, settlement on reservations, religious intolerance, economic deprivation, and psychological despair to Indian peoples. Our ancestors were forced to give up their lands and way of life for a position on the lower rungs of American society. The eventual payoff, after assimilation and acculturation, was participation in the American Dream. By relying on their inner strength; by believing in the foundations of their societies that promoted family, sharing, prayers, hope; and by never giving up, Indian people survived the experience of conquest. Today, nineteen Pueblos, two Apache tribes, and a portion of the Navajo Nation are located on over 8 million acres of New Mexico with an ever-growing population and increasing economic might.

—Veronica E. Velarde Tiller, Jicarilla Apache

Top: Ancestral Pueblo water jar from Tsankawi, ca. 1500.
Bottom: Little Lulu ring probably made at Zuni Pueblo in the 1950s.

The Navajo-Hopi land dispute is a story of the Hopis' and Navajos' claim to ancient rights to the land of their forefathers. Our grandmas said that the Hopi came out of the earth from the Sipapu (earth navel). It is where the Little Colorado River and the Colorado River come together. It is where man emerged into the Fourth World. My uncles speak of how the U.S. government is drawing new lines so the Navajos can use the land. Our grandpa said, "Let the government have it. They will use it up, and when they feel that the land is no longer any use to them, they will leave." It is the Hopi understanding that many will come to try and claim what is Hopi, but in the end the Hopi will still be here, a place near the Sipapu, a place we call home.

— Michael Lacapa, Apache/Hopi/Tewa

"Look down!" I tell my kids when we hike. "Look and see the ancient people of this land. These pieces of clay pottery at our feet and across this land not only held food and water but also the lives of the ancient people of the Mogollon." Pottery stored food, held water, and carried sacred materials. The designs and patterns carried stories. The shapes and forms were created for specific rituals and ceremonies. The images that lie within each vessel were shared mother to daughter. Each vessel carried with it the life of the maker. It is that life that we touch today.

— Michael Lacapa, Apache/Hopi/Tewa

We want to be pure in one way or another. I am a full-blood Navajo. The idea in my mind is a Navajo idea. I use a Navajo blanket, wear Navajo jeans, sing Navajo songs. Taking things for granted, rarely do we look beyond an idea. We accept what our elders tell us without questioning the source or validity of the information. When we look beyond, we find that Navajos have taken freely and responsibly from other tribal groups. Our ceremonies, such as the Mountain Way and peyotism; our arts, such as weaving and sand painting; our clans, the San Juan Pueblo and Coyote Pass People clans, have come to us. When we meet, we learn from one another and grow as a people.

— Rex Lee Jim, Diné

Profaning the sacred began with the weaving of the first Ye'ii rugs and the commercializing of the ii kááh
(dry sandpaintings). There are taboos. Weavers left a *tl'oójigo* (pathway) to the rug's edge to prevent
the closure of their creativity. *Tl'oójigo* is also found on pots and baskets. There were other
controls for *ts'aa'* (basket) weavers, such as the restriction of having to complete
ts'aa' before dusk. Women couldn't weave loops while pregnant, for this would
make childbirth difficult. As a result, basketry declined and we acquired
our baskets from the neighboring Paiute. Today, baskets are again
being made but with fewer taboos. Now, new secular art
forms are made by weavers, basket makers, potters,
silversmiths, visual artists, and musicians in an
unfolding of our centuries-old creativity.

— Gloria Emerson, Diné

Carrying basket by Hannah Sampson, Paiute/Southern Moapa, 1932.

Santa Fe chic is a form of penance for Pueblo people. Developers have taken the humble mud home and turned it into a palatial monument to ego and checkbook. Today, the central plaza of our pueblos may be traditional mud but elsewhere on the reservation we have abandoned adobe because of its expense. Wood-frame and mobile homes have appeared. We debate tradition and forget that a home is neither material nor style. In the pueblo, the home belongs not only to the individual but to the community. Our home is open to the community when my daughter finishes school or when my son brings a deer. It is open for the feast and when someone dies. It is open when a tribal official knocks on the door. But this attitude of sharing and belonging has become diluted. Today, isolated single-family homes offer less opportunity for interaction among the people. We turn to the government and we pay for wooden boxes constructed from the same mold. Our separation increases and we lose in the process. And the blinking lights of the huge homes in the surrounding hills shine in mockery of our detachment from each other.

—Anthony Dorame, Tesuque Pueblo

In the traditional Navajo economic system, a man or woman might have traded a pair of moccasins for a bag of corn, perhaps exchanged two head of sheep for a protection prayer, or swapped the use of a jewelry design for a load of firewood. Today's economy benefits mostly people off the reservation. Rugs are no longer woven for the people to use as blankets, clothing, bedding, or for other practical uses. Weavers weave rugs to decorate walls of houses off the reservation, and non-Navajo store owners gain all the monetary profit. These monies leave the reservation and are deposited in banks with main offices in cities off the reservation. When people no longer trade rugs for corn pollen, the weavers lose their knowledge about plant life, and the farmer no longer wants to be responsible for raising his own food or making his own clothing and shelter. When people are no longer independent, interdependency collapses. Farmers know that they can always sign up for welfare, and when they shop at grocery stores non-Navajo owners reap the rewards. These problems in the economic system call for a total restructuring, not only of the economic infrastructure but, more importantly, of the Navajo business mind.

— Rex Lee Jim, Diné

My daughter works with the music festival during Indian Market in August and is excited about the new sounds coming from today's Native American musicians and singers. When she brings the tapes and CDs home for me, she is surprised when I say, "I know that song, that's a Navajo corn-grinding song," or "a buffalo song" or "an old round dance song." Modern artists are taking traditional songs and using contemporary rock, rap, and ska to make new sounds. This isn't a new trend, as Native performers like Louis Ballard and the IAIA chorus in the 1960s took songs from different tribes and cultures and used them in modern Anglo forms. While I enjoy this music, my own community does not allow us to sing or perform our dances outside the pueblo. We are concerned with the language and songs being taken away. This fear is shared by many tribes who are now losing their language. People who do not know the language cannot sing the songs in the proper manner or spirit. Our songs were composed for specific purposes and had spiritual messages. What happens when they are used differently? I wonder if the spirits recognize them.

— Carlotta Penny Bird, Santo Domingo Pueblo

Navajo Germantown pictorial blanket, ca. 1890s.

Tohono O'odham basket, ca. 1900.

Have you heard of the war in America's Southwest? It is a war for water. Much has been written about the struggles between tribal groups prior to Columbus, and much has been documented about the conflicts between the Spanish and Apache. But the opponents in this battle are Arizona's Salt River Project, a lifeline to the Phoenix metro area, and the White Mountain Apache Tribe, first users of the water. It is a war with as yet no victor but with many losers.

— Michael Lacapa, Apache/Hopi/Tewa

How would I, an O'odham, explain biodiversity? Other cultures may regard the air, water, land, plants, and animals as separate elements and develop approaches for protecting these "resources" accordingly. For us, biodiversity is a concept that is all encompassing. We call it the O'odham *Himdag* (Way of Life). In the arid climate of the O'odham, rain is the life force of the *tohono*. Most Tohono O'odham songs and ceremonial prayers beseech and acknowledge the coming of rain. In the *Himdag*, since the rainfall and water are sacred it cannot be treated simply as a commodity to be bought, sold, or traded on the open market. These differences in cultural viewpoints are at the root of the conflict between the desert people and the cities and towns of southern Arizona.

Native Seeds/SEARCH seed bank assists in the conservation of the desert's "genetic library" of varieties of corn, squash, beans, and other crops. Desert crops feed us physically, mentally, and spiritually and have songs, prayers, and ceremonies associated with them. A child planting a traditional crop seed from the seed bank continues the cycle begun hundreds of years ago, a cycle, hopefully, to be continued by a child of the future. The Indian Health Service and O'odham agencies serve traditional foods at the IHS hospital in Sells, Arizona, to provide physical and spiritual strength to patients removed from their accustomed diets and surroundings.

—Angelo Joaquin, Jr., Tohono O'odham

Santo Domingo Pueblo olla, ca. 1890s.

The sound of water gurgling over rocks and pebbles blends with the trill and song of birds in the trees. I am transfixed by nature and sit motionless. Suddenly, I become aware of a man standing quietly watching me. He pulls his blanket around his shoulders. Noticing the puzzled look, he murmurs, "My son. You do not recognize me?" He speaks in Tewa but not the same Tewa I speak. "I was here before you. I also came to this spot many times but it looks much different now. The earth is different. These birds in the trees are strange. The cornfields are empty. The homes are scattered. There are many changes. And the people, are they the same? Do they forget?" I feel uncomfortable. He quietly reaches for an evergreen tree nearby. Uttering a prayer, he gently breaks a twig and hands it to me. "When the branch is broken, the twig cannot survive. Without our language and without our ways, you cannot survive as a people." I squirm. A crow squawks in a tree, and I am jolted from my daydream. The man is gone. Blinking, I notice in my hand a fragrant twig of evergreen.

—Anthony Dorame, Tesuque Pueblo

THE **VOICES**

I'm from Santo Domingo Pueblo. I've worked and lived in many places, but always say "I'm going up home" when I return. My grand-parents' vision for me was to become an educator, and their teachings have provided the founda-tion I continually build on. I am blessed with three children, and recently another role—that of grandmother to a beautiful grand-daughter—has led me to override my fears and accept the opportunity to work with the museum. I cannot be there for her every day so I think about what I want to share with her. My experiences are what I can give.

—Carlotta Penny Bird,
Santo Domingo Pueblo

To outward appearances I am an adult at the end of what is consid-ered youth, yet I feel like a boy. I am in my childhood in terms of inner growth. There seems to be so much to learn, do, and experience. My hope is that when I "grow up" I can look back and see progress in myself. At the end I can say, "At

least I did something." At twenty-eight years of age, I haven't done enough. For now I'll say, "I am a young man from Santa Clara Pueblo, still searching."

—Tony R. Chavarria,
Santa Clara Pueblo

The less traveled road was tempt-ing, and I followed it. In my life, I have earnestly tried to "work" at things that are fun and meaningful and avoid "jobs" along the way. My layers of personal history include teaching in high schools and univer-sities, writing books and articles, painting with oils and acrylics, and working on environmental issues. But I have too often neglected hunt-ing and fishing in the mountains. Along the way, I pushed the books seriously enough to acquire a couple of college degrees. My family is my inspiration and my treasure.

—Anthony Dorame,
Tesuque Pueblo

My father is a farmer, a man of the mountains. My mother is a woman of the gray plains. We live

along the San Juan River and are blessed with great flocks of birds. We struggle with bad irrigation pumps and raise corn and melons under the black cloud of the Four Corners power plant. Since it's diffi-cult to make a living from our small farm plots, we work elsewhere. Trees have been replaced by oil rigs. Open land cut by fences. TV has taken the place of our grandmas. Take my picture quick, while I eat my watermelon.

—Gloria Emerson,
Diné (Navajo)

I write poems, short stories, and plays in the Navajo language. Also, I conduct research and develop cur-ricula for Navajo Community College through the Office of Diné Educational Philosophy. I lecture fre-quently on Navajo issues. I believe that everything I do makes me a better person. I love to read, engage in intelligent discussion, and to enhance my spiritual understand-ing. I thrive within the web of my social connections. I live in Rock Point, Arizona, the place where I grew up herding sheep and sleeping on the job in the shade of the sagebrush and tamarisk bush. I enjoy life!

—Rex Lee Jim,
Diné (Navajo)

I am a member of the Tohono O'odham Nation in southern Arizona and currently serve as the executive director of Native Seeds/SEARCH in Tucson, Arizona. Native Seeds/SEARCH collects and distributes seeds from traditional crops in order to preserve the biodiversity of these crops. I have served as an advisor for several museum exhibits, but this is the first time I have written for one. I approached the challenge with equal amounts of apprehension and excitement. The experience of working with so many outstanding professional Native American writers and museum staff has made a lasting impression on me.

—Angelo Joaquin, Jr.,
Tohono O'odham (Pima)

I am a full-blooded, enrolled member of the Hopi tribe, a member of the Third Mesa Greasewood Clan, and I live in the village of Paaqavi (Bacavi). I am the director of the Hopi Cultural Preservation Office. I come from a family of farmers and shepherds. I have delivered papers at conferences of the American Anthropological Association and the Society of American Archeology. I am a member of the Arizona Archeological Commission, the Colorado Society of Archeologists, and the Arizona State Museum Tribal Advisory Board. I am a graduate of Northern Arizona University with a degree in business administration.

—Leigh J. Kuwanwisiwma,
Hopi

I am *Ts'lea enu*, Michael Lacapa, an artist! I lived with "The People" and now reside in Taylor, Arizona. My mother is of the Bear Clan. My father is of the Spider Clan. I make images in books to tell stories I recall. I play sounds in the canyons that remind me of the wind blowing through the trees. My work is of the things I do as an Apache, as a Hopi, and as a Tewa. In my culture, we are all artists! Just as we breathe, so must we make art.

—Michael Lacapa,
Apache/Hopi/Tewa

I am a *Shiwi,* a Zuni. I was educated on the Zuni Reservation. I would have graduated from the Albuquerque Indian School had it not been for the Second World War. I served in the armed forces in the Pacific and the Mediterranean and was honorably discharged on December 7, 1946. I entered the University of New Mexico in 1951 and earned my M.A. in 1964. I was employed by the United States Department of the Interior, National Park Service, and retired in 1984. I now am employed by the Museum of New Mexico, Laboratory of Anthropology.

—Edmund J. Ladd,
Zuni Pueblo (deceased 1999)

I am a woman from the Gap Bodaway community at the westernmost edge of the Navajo Reservation. I belong to the

THE VOICES

Tábąąhá (Edge of Water) Clan and am born for the *Tł'ízílání* (Manygoats) Clan. *Tódí ch'íínii* (Bitterwater) Clan are my maternal grandparents, and *Kin yaa'áanii* (Towering House) Clan are my paternal grandparents. My parents impressed on me the importance of knowing how "white people" think, so I studied English and linguistics at the University of Arizona. I have enjoyed this unique opportunity to work directly with *Here, Now, and Always,* for and with many Native Americans from the Southwest.

—Lillie Lane,
Diné (Navajo)

I have lived in Santa Clara all my life. I never had to put down roots here, for I grew up from them. My roots are intertwined with those of all the other members of my community. Santa Clara Pueblo is the home of my ancestors, and it is where I belong. From this place I can watch the movement of the clouds across the sky and the changing of the seasons, each cloud and each year different from the last. It

is the place and the people that make me who I am.

—Tessie Naranjo,
Santa Clara Pueblo

Originally from Taos Pueblo, I lived in Santa Fe for fifteen years. I recently returned to my homeland with my husband and my two children. Trained as a museologist at the Institute of American Indian Arts, I have worked in this field for approximately eight years. I am at present appreciating the arts, my children, and my home.

—Paula Rivera,
Taos Pueblo

I was born in Shiprock, New Mexico, on the Navajo Nation. My family and home community have always been a major influence. I am an associate professor of English at the University of Kansas in Lawrence. Although my husband, children, and grandchildren are here also, we consider "home" to be Navajo Country. My family and extended family live in and around Shiprock. Over the years, I've

learned that we are truly blessed to have a "homeland" that composes our strong identity, history, language, and spiritual beliefs. It teaches us the ways of *Hózhó,* beauty.

—Luci Tapahonso,
Diné (Navajo)

As descendants of traditional Jicarilla Apache chiefs and religious leaders, my parents, Rebecca Monarco Martinez and Albert Velarde, Jr., expected us to maintain the highest standards in the ways of the Jicarilla Apache. We were taught to speak our language and to protect our cultural integrity for all time to the best of our abilities. We were educated in the ways of the white man, without which we could not live up to our tribal obligations. I have a doctor of philosophy degree in history from the University of New Mexico and own Tiller Research, Inc., and BowArrow Publishing Company.

—Veronica E. Velarde Tiller,
Jicarilla Apache

ACKNOWLEDGMENTS

The impetus for this book came from Duane Anderson, director of the Museum of Indian Arts and Culture (MIAC) and the Laboratory of Anthropology in Santa Fe, New Mexico. Anderson's enthusiasm for the exhibition *Here, Now, and Always,* which was already in place when he took over his position as director, and his appreciation of the desire of hundreds of museum visitors to carry home these words, led him to inspire the team that worked on the book, to raise the necessary funding, and to fast-track a project that numerous people had dreamed about for many years.

The real creators of *Here, Now, and Always* are the Native Americans whose words and voices are recorded in these pages and who helped create the exhibition on which the book is based. But other writers made invaluable, if less visible, contributions. For my text in this volume I drew on several sources, most notably the writings of Bruce Bernstein and Sarah Schlanger, former director and archaeology curator, respectively, at MIAC. They composed exhibition and brochure text and compiled extensive notebooks detailing the thinking and research that went into planning the exhibition. Schlanger, along with the staff of Museum of New Mexico Press, also prepared a prospectus for an initial approach to this book. I have relied a great deal on her input and have credited her wherever she is quoted directly. Tony R. Chavarria, current curator of ethnology at MIAC, provided research assistance and production coordination, assisted with the selection of items to be illustrated, worked with the photographer to record them, and helped write the captions. I am grateful for his calm capability, unflagging enthusiasm, and gentle humor. Blair Clark, and other photographers named in the credits, created the beautiful object photographs in the book. Bruce Bernstein gave of his time and experience,

lent his notes and essays, and met with me several times to describe the genesis of the exhibition.

At the Museum of New Mexico Press, Editorial Director Mary Wachs made this book a reality. Mary Sweitzer designed the book and managed its production.

Key contributors to the exhibition *Here, Now, and Always,* on which this book is based, included MIAC staff members and Native consultants: Kerry Boyd (exhibition designer), Carol Cooper (museum educator), Ted Jojola (Isleta Pueblo, consulting curator), Edmund J. Ladd (Zuni Pueblo, curator of ethnology), Steve Lekson (curator of archaeology), Rina Swentzell (Santa Clara Pueblo, consulting curator), Bruce Bernstein, Tony R. Chavarria (Santa Clara Pueblo, assistant curator), Lillie Lane (Diné, curator), Paula Rivera (Taos Pueblo, assistant curator), Sarah Schlanger (curator of archaeology), and Tessie Naranjo (Santa Clara Pueblo, consulting curator), and Gloria Emerson (Diné, consulting curator). The museum also benefited from the assistance of an extraordinary group of Native elders and scholars who served on the museum's Advisory Panel, including Steven Begay (Diné), Larry Benallie (Diné), Walter Dasheno (Santa Clara Pueblo), Agnes Dill (Isleta Pueblo), James Hena (Tesuque Pueblo), Julia Herrera (Laguna Pueblo), Angelo Joaquin, Jr. (Tohono O'odham), Brenda Julian (Jicarilla Apache), Michael Kabotie (Hopi), Michael Lacapa (Hopi/Apache/Tewa), Gloria Lomaheftewa (Hopi/Choctaw), Geronima Montoya (San Juan Pueblo), Milford Nahohai (Zuni Pueblo), Edgar Perry (White Mountain Apache), Lydia Pesata (Jicarilla Apache), Joe Sando (Jemez Pueblo), Jim Trujillo (Taos Pueblo), and Lonnie Vigil (Nambé Pueblo). Roseann Willink, of the Language Department of the University of New Mexico, checked the Navajo spellings in the text.

—Joan K. O'Donnell

ILLUSTRATION CREDITS

All object photographs (catalog numbers below) are by Blair Clark, unless otherwise noted,
and are © Museum of Indian Arts and Culture/Laboratory of Anthropology.
All historical photographs are courtesy of the Photo Archives of the Museum of New Mexico.

Page 12: Map by Deborah Reade. 12: Photo and © Sarah Schlanger 1993. 14: Photo and © Sarah Schlanger.
15 top: Photo and © Sarah Schlanger 1997. 15 bottom: Cat. no. 43804. 17 inset: Photo and © Sarah Schlanger
1991. 17: Photo and © Sarah Schlanger 1996. 18 bottom left: Cat. no. 54364a,b. 18 top: Photo and © Sarah
Schlanger 1978. 18 bottom right: Cat. nos. 8822 (Mesa Verde black-on-white, 1200 - 1300), 43336 (Chaco
black-on-white, 1050 - 1300), 46550 (Gallup black-on-white, 1000 - 1100), 54389 (Mesa Verde black-on-white,
1200 - 1300), 19616 (Mesa Verde black-on-white, 1200 - 1300). 19 top: Cat. no. 8366. 19 bottom: Photo and
© Sarah Schlanger 1988. 20: Photo and © Sarah Schlanger 1987. 21: Photo and © Sarah Schlanger 1991.
22: Cat. no. 35464. 22 top: Cat. no. 51300, photo by Murrae Haynes. 23 bottom: Cat. no. 1747. 24: Photo and
© Sarah Schlanger 1997. 25: Cat. no. 43321, photo by Mary Peck. 26: Photo and © Sarah Schlanger 1989.
27 left: Cat. nos. 308, 494, 8490, 8649, 8659, 25873, 25879, 26556, 38496, 39025, 43193, 44934,
52637, 54663. 27 right: Education Collection. 28: Cat. nos. 234g (pendant fragments), 236a,b,c,f,g,h, 237,
17921 (drilled pendant), 25947 9 (raw stone), 27151a - d (cylindrical beads). 29: Cat. no. 53943. 30: Cat. nos.
586, 42390. 31 top: Cat. nos. 54773, 53776, 53778, 53779. 31 bottom: Cat. no. 49995, photo by Murrae
Haynes. 33: Cat. no. 55671. 34: Photo and © Sarah Schlanger. 35: Cat. no. 24271. 36: Photo and © Sarah
Schlanger 1989. 37: Cat. nos. 31937, 36879, 36880. 39: Cat. nos. 14548, 42347, 42348. 40 inset: Cat. no.
23981a,b. 40: MNM neg. no. 77471, photo by Harold Kellog. 42: MNM neg. no. 21621, photo by H. F.
Robinson. 43: Cat. nos. 3, 11000, 48669. 44: Cat. no. 10997. 45: Cat. no. 52883. 46: MNM neg. no. 72606,
photo by Herman S. Hoyt. 47: neg. no. 120405, photo by Tyler Dingee. 49: MNN neg. no. 2091. 51: MNM neg.
no. 56151. 52: MNM neg. no. 31961, photo by Edward S. Curtis. 54: Education Collection. 57: MNM neg. no.
100358, photo by Ferenz Fedor. 58: Cat. nos. 10811, 40814, 1412, 7597, 11413. 59: Cat. no. 9856. 60:
Cat. no. 31959, photo by Douglas Kahn. 61: Cat. no. 18796. 62: Cat. no. 36619. 63: Cat. no. 9051. 64 Cat.
no. 50429. 65: Cat. no. 26233. 66: Cat. nos. 7383, 23194, 36971. 67: Cat. no. 11059. 68: Cat. no. 51404.
69: Cat. no. 10662, photo by Douglas Kahn. 70-1: Courtesy Monty Roessel © Monty Roessel. 72: Cat. no.
53628. 74: Cat. no. 23600. 75 top: Cat. no. 19513. 75 bottom: Cat. no. 51640. 76: Cat. no. 9972. 79: Cat.
no. 9316. 80: Cat. no. 23455. 81: Cat. no. 47724.

We must remember the worlds
　　　our ancestors traveled.
Always wear the songs they gave us.
　　　Remember we are made of prayers.
Now we leave wrapped in blankets
　　　of love and wisdom.

　　　　　　　— Luci Tapahonso, Diné